CHI KUNG

HEALTH & MARTIAL ARTS

氣功与應用

BY DR. YANG JWING-MING

DISCLAIMER

The author(s) and publisher of this material are NOT RESPONSIBLE in any manner whatsoever for any injury which may occur through reading or following the instructions in this material.

The activities, physical and otherwise, described in this material may be too strenuous or dangerous for some people, and the reader(s) should consult a physician before engaging in them.

© YANG'S MARTIAL ARTS ASSOCIATION (YMAA), 1985, 1987, 1988

THIRD PRINTING

ISBN: 0-940871-00-9
Library of Congress No: 87-050144

Printed in the United States of America

YANG'S MARTIAL ARTS ASSOCIATION (YMAA)

38 HYDE PARK AVENUE

JAMAICA PLAIN, MASSACHUSETTS 02130

ACKNOWLEDGEMENTS

Thanks to John Gilbert Jones, Russell Steinberg, and Kenneth Silva for general help with the work. Thanks to the editor, Michael Braun, and special thanks to Alan Dougall for proofing the manuscript and contributing many valuable suggestions and discussions. Thanks to John Casagrande, Jr. for the drawings and cover design. Thanks also to Angie Adams and John Dufresne for typesetting.

ABOUT THE
AUTHOR

Dr. Yang Jwing-Ming was born in Taiwan, Republic of China, in 1946. He started his *Wushu (Kung Fu)* training at the age of fifteen under the Shaolin White Crane (*Pai Huo* division) Master Cheng Gin-Gsao. In thirteen years of study (1961-1974), under Master Cheng, Dr. Yang became an expert in White Crane defense and attack, which includes both the use of barehands and of various weapons such as saber, staff, spear, trident, and two short rods. With the same master he also studied White Crane *Chin Na*, massage, and herbal treatment. At the age of sixteen Dr. Yang began the study of *Tai Chi Chuan* (Yang style) under Master Kao Tao. After learning from Master Kao, Dr. Yang continued his study and research of *Tai Chi* Chuan with several masters in Taipei. In Taipei he became qualified to teach *Tai Chi*. He has mastered the *Tai Chi* barehand sequence, pushing hands, the two-man fighting sequence, *Tai Chi* sword, *Tai Chi* saber, and internal power development.

When Dr. Yang was eighteen years old he entered Tamkang College in Taipei Hsien to study Physics. In college, he began the study of Shaolin Long Fist (*Chang Chuan*) with Master Li Mao-Ching at the Tamkang College Kuoshu Club (1964-1968), and eventually became an assistant instructor under Master Li. In 1971 he completed his M.S. degree in Physics at the National Taiwan University, and then served in the Chinese Air Force from 1971-1972. In the service, Dr. Yang taught Physics at the Junior Academy of the Chinese Air Force while also teaching *Wushu*. After being honorably discharged in 1972, he returned to Tamkang College to teach Physics and resume study under Master Li Mao-Ching. From Master Li, Dr. Yang learned Northern style *Wushu*, which includes both barehand (especially kicking) techniques and numerous weapons.

In 1974, Dr. Yang came to the United States to study Mechanical Engineering at Purdue University. At the request of a few students, Dr. Yang began to teach *Kung Fu* which resulted in the foundation of the Purdue University Chinese *Kung Fu* Research Club in the spring of 1975. While at Purdue, Dr. Yang also taught college-credited courses in *Tai Chi Chuan*. In May of 1978, he was awarded a Ph.D. in Mechanical Engineering from Purdue.

Currently, Dr. Yang and his family reside in Massachusetts. In January of 1984, he gave up his engineering career to devote more time to research, writing, and teaching at Yang's Martial Arts Academy in Boston.

In summary, Dr. Yang has been involved in Chinese *Wushu (Kung Fu)* for more than twenty years. During this time, he has spent thirteen years learning

Shaolin White Crane (*Pai Huo*), Shaolin Long Fist (*Chang Chuan*), and *Tai Chi Chuan*. Dr. Yang has sixteen years of instructional experience: seven years in Taiwan, five years at Purdue University, two years in Houston, Texas, and two years in Boston, Massachusetts.

Dr. Yang has published four volumes on martial arts:

1. *Shaolin Chin Na*; Unique Publications, Inc., 1980.
2. *Shaolin Long Fist Fung Fu*; Unique Publications, Inc., 1981.
3. *Yang Style Tai Chi Chuan*; Unique Publications, Inc., 1981.
4. *Introduction to Ancient Chinese Weapons*; Unique Publications, Inc., 1985.

In addition, Dr. Yang has published the videotape "*Yang Style Tai Chi Chuan and Its Applications*", Yang's Martial Arts Academy, 1984.

Dr. Yang plans to publish a number of additional books including:

1. *Northern Shaolin Sword*
2. *Advanced Yang Style Tai Chi Chuan*
3. *Dissection of Shaolin Chin Na - Instructor's Manual*
4. *Northern Shaolin Staff*
5. *Tai Chi Chuan and Health*

Also several videotapes have been scheduled for publication:

1. "*Shaolin Long Fist Kung Fu–Lien Bu Chaun*"
2. "*Shaolin Long Fist Kung Fu–Gung Li Chuan*"
3. "*Shaolin Long Fist Kung Fu–Yi Lu Mei Fu*"
4. "*Shaolin Long Fist Kung Fu–Shaw Fu Ien*"
5. "*Shaolin Long Fist Kung Fu–Shih Tzu Tan*"
6. "*Yang Style Tai Chi Sword and Its Applications*"

PREFACE

"*Kung Fu*" in Chinese means an achievement or activity which requires time, energy, and patience. *Chi Kung* (pronounced chee goong) means the *Kung Fu* of internal energy circulation. *Chi* has been known for more than a decade by the Western world, but it still remains a mysterious or fuzzy concept to most Westerners and even to many *Chi Kung* practitioners. Many people have experienced health benefits from learning *Chi Kung*, although very few of them really understand the principles or theory behind it, the relationship between *Chi Kung* and acupuncture, or the connection between *Chi Kung* and the martial arts. The author hopes that this volume, which specializes in *Chi Kung*, will help to dispel the mystery and thus benefit more people.

In this book, the first chapter will explain the general concept of *Chi Kung*, its history, its relationship to health and to the martial arts. The second chapter will introduce *Wai Dan* (external elixir), or techniques to promote external/internal local *Chi* circulation. The history of the creator of Shaolin *Wai Dan*, Da Mo, and the book he wrote on the subject, the *Yi Gin Ching*, will also be discussed. The third chapter will present the main training of Chi Kung called *Nei Dan* (internal elixir), or internal/internal *Dan Tien Chi* circulation, which was developed by the Taoists and Buddhists. The fourth chapter will explain the use of *Chi Kung* to improve and maintain health. And finally, the fifth chapter will discuss in general the application of *Chi Kung* to the martial arts. An additional volume will be necessary to cover the principles and methods of training in detail. The author hopes to be able to do this in the near future. Those who wish further information are referred to the author's books *Yang Style Tai Chi Chuan* for specifics on that system, and to *Shaolin Chin Na* for information on cavity press.

TABLE OF CONTENTS

CHAPTER 1
INTRODUCTION

1-1. General Introduction

Chi Kung, also properly called *Nei Kung*(Internal *Kung Fu*), is a practice that has been used by the Chinese people for thousands of years--both to improve and maintain their health and to develop greater power for the martial arts. *Kung* means work in Chinese, and *Chi* means the energy that circulates within the body, so *Chi Kung* means the development of the body's energy circulation, both to increase it and to control it.

Although it has been widely practiced for a very long time, many people are confused about *Chi Kung*, even in China, and many doubt the possibility of internal energy development, or even the existence of *Chi*. There are several reasons for this. Until as recently as 50 years ago most experts in *Chi Kung* would only teach their own sons or a few people they trusted, so that the knowledge was not very widespread. Many of the techniques were developed and cultivated by Buddhist or Taoist monks who would not spread their teachings outside their own temples. Because most people were ignorant of *Chi Kung*, it has been superstitiously regarded as magic. Another reason for the confusion about *Chi Kung* is that some people learned incorrect methods and so experienced no effects from the training, or even injured themselves. This has resulted in people being afraid to try *Chi Kung* if they heard of the injuries, or being scornful if they heard of the lack of success of practitioners.

The reader should understand that there is a theory behind *Chi Kung*. This is the body of Chinese medicine with a history going back thousands of years. The most important books describing *Chi* and its actions are the *Chi Far Lun* (or Theory of Chi's Variations), which explains the relationship of *Chi* and nature, and the *Gin Lou Lun* (or Theory of Chi Channels and Branches), which describes the *Chi's* circulation throughout the human body (*"Gin"* means channel, *"Lou"* refers to the subchannels that branch out from them). A channel is a major connector of the internal organs with the rest of the body. These channels frequently are co-located with major nerves or arteries, but the correspondence is not complete, and it seems that they are neither nerves nor blood vessels, but simply the main routes for *Chi*. There are twelve main channels and two major vessels, which are also commonly called channels. Along these channels are found the "cavities" *(Hsueh)*, sometimes known as acupuncture points, which can be used to stimulate the entire system.

Chi Kung is also based upon the theory of *Yin* and *Yang* which describes the relationship of complementary qualities such as soft and hard, female and male, dark and light, or slow and fast. According to this theory nature strives to harmonize complements so that things are neutral or balanced. Since people are part of nature, they should strive to maintain themselves in balance as well.

Included in *Yin/Yang* theory is the theory of the five elements or phases: *Gin* (metal), *Moo* (wood), *Sui* (water), *For* (fire), and *Tu* (earth), which are somewhat different from the old European four elements: fire, air, water, earth. Again, since people are part of nature, they participate in the interplay of the elements.

According to Chinese medicine there are two ways to study health and illness: externally called "*Wai Shain Gieh Por*", and internally called "*Nei Shih Kung Fu*". *Wai Shain Gieh Por* is a way to understand the human body by dissection or by acting physically on the body and observing the results, as in modern laboratory experiments. In *Nei Shih Kung Fu* the researcher learns by introspection. He observes his own body and sensations and develops his medical knowledge this way.

The Western world has specialized almost exclusively in *Wai Shain* and has considered *Nei Shih* as "unscientific", although in recent years this attitude has been changing markedly among the general populace if not within the medical profession.

The first step of *Nei Shih Kung Fu* came from observing the correspondence between the way people feel and the changes in nature, and discovering the *Chi's* variations. "Nature" here includes periodic cycles (*Tien Shih*) such as air pressure, wind direction, season, humidity, and time of day. It also includes geographical features (*Di Li*) such as altitude, distance from the equator, and distance from large bodies of water, such as the ocean or a lake. These empirical observations led to the conclusion that *Chi* circulation is related to nature, and led to a search for ways for people to harmonize with the natural variations.

In addition *Chi* was also observed to be closely related to human affairs (*Zen Shih*). This includes the relationship of *Chi* to sound, emotion, and food. Because *Chi* flow is controlled by the brain, any agitation of the brain by emotion will affect the *Chi* circulation. The sounds people made in various situations were also observed. For example in cold weather the sound *"shih"* is used combined with keeping the limbs close to the body and breathing deeply to help keep warm. The pain from cuts can be relieved by making the sound *"shiu"* and blowing air into the cut. The sound *"shiu"* helps to stop the bleeding and calm the liver, and this organ's relaxation in turn relieves the pain. The sound *"hai"* is used to increase the person's working strength. The sound *"ha"* will help to relieve fevers the same way a dog's panting helps it to bear the heat. From all these observations it was concluded that different sounds can relieve the pressure or strain on different organs, and since inner organs were related to the channels, the *Chi* circulation was affected as well. The relationship of *Chi* with food is illustrated by the fact that drinking too much alcohol or eating too much deep fried foods will strain the liver and thus will affect the *Chi* circulation in the liver channel.

After a long period of observation people began to understand that *Chi* circulation is important to one's health, and they began to investigate ways to improve the *Chi's* circulation. Methods were found and forms were created that proved effective, which was the beginning of *Chi Kung*.

1-2. Historical Survey

There have been four major divisions or schools of *Chi Kung* practice and theory: the Confucians, the Physicians, the Buddhist monks, and the Taoists. These groups are not mutually exclusive, since a physician studying the workings of *Chi* in his practice might also be a Confucian or Taoist. However, the works we have are usually identifiable as belonging to one particlar group. The Confucians were primarily interested in the working of human society rather than in withdrawal and self perfection. For them the purpose of *Chi Kung* is to make people more fit to fulfill their function. They included many famous artists and scholars, and their views on *Chi Kung* are frequently expressed in poetry. The most famous of these poets were Li Pai, Su Tung-Pou, and Bai Gue-Yi. Su Tung-Pou was the co-author with Shen Tsun-Chung of *Su Shen Lian Fan* (or Good Prescriptions of Su and Shen.) The physicians were not specifically aligned with any philosophical group, although their work often has recognizable Taoist influence. Their work is distinguished by its emphasis on discussing the balance of *Chi*. The Buddhist monks emphasized becoming free from the suffering of existence through awareness. Their primary method was still meditation with breathing directed toward stilling the mind. Although considerable *Chi* circulation was developed, it was not the primary goal. The Taoists are associated with withdrawal from society to perfect the self and achieve immortality. To do this they used *Chi Kung* and alchemy, and these two are frequently discussed together. In fact two terms used in this book, *"Wai Dan"* and *"Nei Dan"*, which describe methods of improving *Chi* circulation, originally meant the alchemical elixir of immortality.

Records from before the Han dynasty are very fragmented and much of the history of the period is conjecture. Traditionally the history of *Chi* theory begins with the beginning of Chinese medicine in the reign of the Yellow Emperor, Huang Di (2690-2590 B.C.). The book that is the theoretical foundation for Chinese medicine to the present day, the *Nei Ching Su Wen*, (or Classic on Internal Medicine), is attributed to Huang Di, but modern scholars now believe it to be a work of the Han dynasty.

The Yi Ching, (or Book of Changes), on the other hand, is a very old book, believed to date before 2400 B.C. It discusses all the variations of nature in compact form. Natural forces are represented by the eight trigrams, and these are combined into 64 hexagrams. These figures have permeated every aspect of Chinese culture, and it is not surprising that the eight trigrams are used to describe the circulation of *Chi* in the body.

By the time of the Shang dynasty (1766-1154 B.C.) people used stone probes called *"Bian Shih"* (Fig. 1-1) to stimulate cavities on the channels which affected the *Chi* circulation and relieved pain. They had already discovered that a sharp instrument was better for stimulating pressure points than just the fingers.

In the sixth century B.C. the philosopher Lao Tzu (Li Erh) described breathing techniques for increasing the life span in his classic the *Tao Te Ching* (or Classic on the Virtue of the *Tao*)(especially see Chapter 10). This was the first record of using breathing techniques to increase *Chi* circulation and thereby to increase the length of life.

The *Shih Gi* (Historical Record) shows that by the Spring and Autumn and Warring States periods (770-221 B.C.) more complete methods of breath training had been evolved.

（河南殷墟安陽出土）石砭

Fig. 1-1. *Bian Shih* Found at Henan Province

About 300 B.C. the Taoist philosopher Chuang Tzu described the relationship between breathing and health in his book *Nan Hua Ching*. It states: "The men of old breathed clear down to their heels.." This confirms that a breathing method of *Chi* circulation was being used by some Taoists at that time.

During the Chin and Han dynasties (221 B.C. to 220 A.D.) several books related to *Chi Kung* were written. The *Nan Ching* (or Classic on Disorders) by the famous doctor Bian Chiueh describes using breathing to increase *Chi* circulation. The *Han Su Yi Wun Tzu* describes four methods of *Chi Kung* training. The *Gin Guey Yao Liueh* by Chang Chung-Gien describes using breathing and acupuncture to maintain good *Chi* flow. The *Chou Yi Chan Ton Chi* by Wei Bo-Yang describes the relationship of humans with natural forces and with *Chi*. During this time also anatomical knowledge grew through the dissection of bodies. The structure of the human body in relation to the channel and nervous systems was understood better than before, and the existence of *Chi* circulation gained wider acceptance.

During the Gin dynasty in the third century A.D., the famous physician Hua Tor used acupuncture for anesthesia in surgery. In addition he spread the Taoist Juan Gin method, which imitated the five animals: tiger, deer, monkey, bear, and bird to generate local *Chi* circulation. This was a form of *Wai Dan* and was called *Wu Chin Si* (or five animal sport). The physician Gar Hung mentions using the mind to guide and increase the flow of *Chi* in his *Bao Poh Tzu*.

Sometime in the period of 420 to 581 A.D. Tao Hung-Gin compiled the *Yang Shen Yen Ming Lu* which records many *Chi Kung* techniques for improving health.

During the Liang dynasty (502-557 A.D.) Da Mo, a Buddhist monk, arrived at the Shaolin temple (see Chapter 2 for Da Mo's history). Da Mo saw that the monks were weak and could do very little and was so disturbed by this that he shut himself away to ponder the problem. He stayed in seclusion for nine years. When he emerged he had written two books, one of which, the *Yi Gin*

Ching (or Muscle Development Classic) still survives. The exercises in this book are a form of *Wai Dan* (external-internal *Chi Kung*) using concentration to develop local *Chi* and increase the *Chi* circulation. The monks practiced these methods and found that they greatly increased their power. This training was integrated into the martial arts forms and was the first known application of *Chi Kung* to the martial arts.

The Shaolin priests continued developing these methods and came up with five sets of forms that imitate the movements of animals known for their fighting ability. These were the tiger, the leopard, the dragon, the snake, and the crane. These animal names are still found in *Kung Fu* styles.

Development of *Chi Kung* methods and theory continued during the Sui and Tang dynasties (581-907 A.D.). Chow Yun-Fan compiled the *Chu Bin Yun Hou Lu* which is a veritable encyclopedia of methods. He lists 260 different ways of increasing the flow of *Chi*. The *Chen Gin Fan* by Sun Ssu-Mao describes a method of guiding *Chi*, introduces the use of the six sounds (see Chapter 4) and their relationship with the internal organs, and also introduces a collection of massage techniques called Lao Tzu's 49 Massage Techniques. *Wai Tai Mi Yao* by Wang Tor discusses the use of breathing and herbal therapies for disorders of *Chi* circulation.

During the period 960 to 1368 A.D. (the Sung, Gin, and Yuan dynasties) several works of interest were written. *Yang Shen Gieh* by Chang An-Tao discusses *Chi Kung* practice. *Zu Men Shih Shih* by Chang Tzu-Huo uses *Chi Kung* to cure external injuries such as cuts and sprains. *Lan Shih Mi Chan* by Li Gou uses *Chi Kung* and herbal remedies for internal disorders. *Ge Tzu Yu Lun* by Chu Dan-Si provides a theoretical explanation for the use of *Chi Kung* in curing sickness.

It was during the Sung dynasty (960-1279 A.D.) that Chang San-Feng is reputed to have created *Tai Chi Chuan* at Wu Dan Mountain. *Tai Chi* is a martial form of *Nei Dan Chi Kung* which builds the energy from the *Dan Tien*, which is a spot in the lower abdomen one and a half inches below the navel. One starts with the "Small Circulation" in the torso and head, then extends it to the "Grand Circulation" in the whole body, and then this energy is applied to martial uses.

In 1026 A.D. the famous Brass Man (a hollow brass dummy with the channels marked and holes in the cavity locations, see Fig. 1-2) was built by Wang Wei-Yi. This great accomplishment helped people to organize acupuncture theory more systematically.

From then until the Ching dynasty the existence of *Chi*, its benefits to health, and its usefulness to the martial arts continued to gain wider acceptance among the Chinese people. Many ways of increasing *Chi* circulation were developed and practiced. For example General Yeuh Fei who lived in the Southern Sung dynasty (1177-1279 A.D.) is reputed to have been the creator of many *Chi Kung* styles. It is said that General Yeuh Fei, seeing that his soldiers were weak, used the Da Mo *Yi Gin Ching* exercises as a foundation and modified it into *Shih Er Dun Gin* or Twelve Pieces of Brocade (later simplified into *Ba Dun Gin* or Eight Pieces of Brocade) to train his soldiers. A later development of the *Shih Er Dun Gin* was *Hsing I* as well as *Liu Ho Ba Fa*.

There are several other styles of *Chi Kung* created during this period that are still used for training by a few people. The martial artists of the Er Mei Division, located at Er Mei Mountain in Sichuan Province, still use their *Fu Bu Kung* (Tiger Step *Kung*) and *Shih Er Chuang* (Twelve Postures). Another

Fig. 1-2. "Brass Man" by Wang Wei-Yi

style rarely used today, but in use before the revolution was *Giaou Far Kung* (Beggar *Kung*) which was practiced by beggars to enable them to withstand a life filled with exposure to the elements and irregular meals. However, this style has nearly died out now.

During the Ming and Ching dynasties (1368-1911 A.D.) the publication of written works on *Chi Kung* continued. *Chi Ling Ba Mei Kou* by Li Shih-Tsin discusses the relationship of *Chi Kung* with the channels. *Bao Shen Mi Yao* by Tso Yun-Bai covers moving and still *Chi Kung. Yang Shen Huo Yu* by Chen Gi-Zu discusses the three essences *Gien* (sperm), *Chi* (internal energy) and *Shen* (spirit) and how to protect and preserve them. For men both excessive retention of sperm and excess dispersion are bad for the health, so one's sex life must be carefully regulated according to one's constitution and age. *Yi Fan Gi Gieh* by Wong Fan-Yen is a review and summary of previously published material. Wang Tzu-Yun's *Nei Kung Tuo Shou* presents the Twelve Pieces of

Brocade exercise, and explains the idea of using both moving and still types of *Chi Kung*.

The well known *Ba Kua Chuan* (Eight Trigrams Fist) was created during the Ching dynasty (1644-1911 A.D.) and is still practiced today. Another popular style, called *For Long Kung* (Fire Dragon *Kung*), was created toward the end of the Ming dynasty (c. 1640 A.D.) by the *Tai Yang* division, and is occasionally used for health purposes. Many other styles or methods have been used, but most have died out, or are known to very few.

Since 1911 so many books have been written in China that the author can only refer the reader to the bookstores. The *Chi Kung* methods most widely known today are *Tai Chi Chuan, Ba Kua Chuan, Hsing I Chuan*, and *Liu Ho Ba Fa*, which are essentially martial arts, and *Shih Er Dun Gin, Ba Dun Gin, Yi Gin Ching*, and *Wu Chin Si*, which are strictly health exercises.

1-3. General Principles

In order to understand *Chi Kung*, the reader must understand several concepts. The first of these is *Chi*.

Chi is the foundation of all Chinese medical theory and *Chi Kung*. It corresponds to the Greek *"pneuma"* and the Sanskrit *"prana"*, and is considered to be the vital force and energy flow in all living things. There is no western definition of *Chi*. However, according to the experience of *Chi Kung* practitioners, *Chi* can be best explained as a type of energy very much like electricity, which flows through the human or animal body. When this circulation becomes stagnant or stops, the person or animal will become ill or die. *Chi* can also be explained as a medium of sensing or feeling.

For example, when a person's arm is hurt, the *Chi* flow in the nerves of the arm will be disturbed and stimulated to a higher energy state. This higher energy potential will cause the *Chi* to flow to a lower energy area, especially the brain, which is extremely sensitive to disturbances in the energy flow. This causes the sensation of pain. In addition, the difference in energy potential will cause the flow of blood to increase in that area to begin repairing the damage. Therefore, *Chi*, the nervous system, the *Chi* channels, and the brain are intimately related to each other and can not be separated.

The second concept the reader should know is that of *Chi* channels, which circulate *Chi* throughout the body. For the most part the main *Chi* channels are found with the arteries and nerves. A glance into any anatomy book will show the reader that large sheaves of nerve fibers accompany the arteries throughout the body. The channels do also. Like the arteries and nerves, they are protected by the body's musculature, so that they are hard to affect directly. There is one spot on the body where a channel is very exposed, and that is the funny bone. This spot is called *Shaohai* in acupuncture and belongs to the Hand *Shaoyin* Heart Channel, and here the channel and median nerve system coincide. A light tap will numb the entire forearm, which demonstrates the extreme sensitivity of the channels, as well as the control they exert throughout the body. Just as the arteries have branches which supply the tissues and organs with blood and carry away waste, the channels have branches (called *"Lou"*) to supply the body with *Chi* and to carry messages to the brain and organs. As mentioned above, this energy circulation system is under the control of the mind, whether one is aware of this or not.

There are twelve main channels and two major vessels in the human body. These twelve channels (actually pairs of channels, one on either side of the body) are related to different internal organs. When the *Chi* is stagnant in one channel, the corresponding organ will be disordered. One of the major techniques of acupuncture is to stimulate the channel with a needle. This increases or lessens the circulation of *Chi*, and helps bring the malfunctioning organ back into balance. The two major vessels are the *Ren Mei* or Conception Vessel, which runs down the center of the body in front, and the *Du Mei* or Governing Vessel, which runs down the center of the back and the head.

The third concept the reader should understand is that of acupuncture points, which are also called "cavities" *(Hsueh)*. Along each of the channels (as well as elsewhere on the body) are spots where the protective muscle is less thick than usual or the channel is closer to the surface. These spots, which are called cavities because they can often be felt as small depressions or concavities, are more sensitive than other parts of the body. These are the spots used for acupuncture, and they are also points of attack in the martial arts. Acupuncture recognizes more than 700 cavities, although only 108 cavities are used by the martial artists. The application of power to one of the 108 cavities can result in pain, numbness of some part of the body, damage to one of the body's internal organs, unconsciousness, or even death. Of these 108 cavities, 36 are death cavities. That is, one strike can damage an internal organ, causing death. For example, the cavity on the heart channel found in the armpit, if struck, can shock the heart so severely that it goes into fatal spasms. The 72 remaining cavities are not death cavities, but striking them can cause numbness or unconsciousness, provided exactly the right spot is hit at the right time.

The fourth concept the reader should know is that the circulation of *Chi* is governed by the time of day and the season of the year. The *Chi* is circulating within the body from conception to death, but the part of the body that is the main focus changes around the clock. However, *Chi* circulates continuously within the two major vessels without being affected by time. Because of the variability of *Chi* circulation, it is essential that the student be knowledgeable about it to be able to use it effectively.

The most important thing to remember is that everything is controlled by the mind. Western science has proven that we use only 30 to 40 percent of our brain capacity. If a person could train himself to use more than this amount, he would be a genius. Science believes that this can be done through meditation and concentration training. It is well documented that a hypnotized person can do things that are far beyond what is possible for him when in a normal state. Meditation is a form of self-hypnosis that can lead you toward this sort of increased performance.

In *Chi Kung* training the mind controls the flow of *Chi*, just as it controls other body functions. Everyone has experienced ways in which his mind causes reactions in his body. Thinking about frightening things can make you sweat. Thinking of a tense situation can cause you to tense up all your muscles so much that your whole body becomes sore. In this case your mind caused a chemical reaction, i.e. the generation of acid in your tight muscles. Your mind can also relax your body just by thinking about it. Many people are using this approach to control their pulse or blood pressure without drugs.

In *Chi Kung* training concentration is the key to success. By concentrating attention on the abdomen and doing certain exercises, *Chi* is generated and circulated throughout the body. This leads to the development of extra energy and its more efficient use, allowing the martial artist to strike with tremendous power and to resist the penetration of an opponent's power into his body. The amount of *Chi* that can be generated is determined largely by the person's ability to concentrate.

There are several common ways to raise *Chi* to a higher energy state. The first way is called *Wai Dan*. In this method, *Chi* is stimulated at a particular location in the body by continued muscular exertion combined with concentration. For example, if a person holds his arms extended in one position for several minutes, the shoulders will become very warm from the *Chi* accumulation. When the tension is relaxed this higher energy will flow to places with a lower state. *Wai Dan* exercises have been in use in China for many centuries. *Wai Dan* was later coordinated with martial techniques by the Shaolin monks. Chapter 2 will explain this method in detail.

The second way of increasing *Chi* circulation is called *"Nei Dan"*. In this method *Chi* is accumulated at the *Dan Tien*, a spot an inch and a half below the navel. When *Chi* has accumulated sufficiently, then the practitioner uses his mind to guide the *Chi* to circulate in the two major vessels. This is called the "Small Circulation". After mastering the Small Circulation, the practitioner will then learn the "Grand Circulation", in which the mind guides the *Chi* flow through all of the twelve channels. This method has been practiced by *Tai Chi* devotees since the thirteenth century. The third chapter will explain *Nei Dan* practice in detail.

The third common way is acupuncture. In acupuncture the needle pierces the skin and musculature layer and stimulates the channel directly. When the channel is stimulated, *Chi* will be built up and circulate in the channel.

The fourth way, which is one that has been used in western medicine, is massage, which stimulates the muscles, building up local *Chi*, which circulates more freely because the muscles relax.

The last common way is friction or rubbing a particular area of the body hard enough to generate heat and stimulate the skin.

There are a few other ways to build up local *Chi*, including slapping the skin and acupressure, which is classified somewhere between massage and acupuncture. Of the five methods mentioned above, *Wai Dan* and *Nei Dan* are the only two that can be applied for martial purposes. The others are for improving health, and will be explained in Chapter 4.

1.4. Popular Martial Styles of Chi Kung Training:

There are two categories of *Chi Kung* training, martial arts and pure *Chi Kung* for health, longevity, and spiritual attainment. Within each category there are many styles. The most popular of the pure *Chi Kung* methods are the *Yi Gin Ching* attributed to Da Mo and *Ba Dun Gin* or Eight Pieces of Brocade. These are discussed in Chapter 2.

The most popular martial arts used for *Chi Kung* are *Tai Chi*, *Hsing Yi*, *Liu Ho Ba Fa*, and *Ba Kua*. Here we will give only a brief review of the history and theory; the student should refer to a book or instructor of each style for deeper study.

Tai Chi Chuan

Tai Chi means "Grand Ultimate", and refers to the *Yin-Yang* concept. *Chuan* means "fist", "boxing", or "style". This boxing style is noted for its slow, relaxed movements. The forms are martial movements, but are performed very slowly, so they appear more like dance than like a martial art. *Tai Chi* is also know as *Shih Shan Shih* or thirteen postures, *Mei Chuan* or Soft Sequence, and *Chang Chuan* or Long Sequence. The thirteen postures refer to the thir-

Fig. 1-3. Wu Chien-Chun

Fig. 1-4. Yang Chen-Fu

teen principle techniques which correspond to the eight trigrams combined with the five phases. These techniques are: Ward-Off, Pluck, Press, Shoulder-Stroke, Roll-Back, Rend, Push, Elbow-Stroke for the eight trigrams, and Advance, Retreat, Dodge and Beware of the Left, Dodge and Beware of the Right, and Hold the Center for the five phases. The soft sequence refers to the relaxed and gentle way in which the forms are performed. The long sequence refers to the fact that the *Tai Chi* barehand sequence takes much longer to perform while containing a larger number of techniques than most other martial styles.

While there is little documentary evidence concerning the origins of *Tai Chi Chuan*, Chang San-Feng is generally credited with creating it at Wu Dan Mountain during the Sung dynasty, basing it on the fighting techniques of the snake and crane combined with internal power. Until the mid-nineteenth century, *Tai Chi Chuan* was a closely guarded secret of the Chen family. At that time Yang Lu-Shan (1780-1873) learned *Tai Chi* from Chen Chang-Shen, the grandmaster of that time. Yang went to Peking and became famous as a martial artist, and passed the system on to his sons, who in turn passed it on to the public. Yang Lu-Shan's second son, Yang-Pan Huo (1837-1890) taught the style to a number of people, including Wu Chun-Yu, whose son Wu Chien-Chun (Fig. 1-3) modified the style and founded the Wu Style of *Tai Chi Chuan*, which is especially popular in Hong Kong, Singapore, and Malaysia. A grandson of Yang Lu-Shan, Yang Cheng-Fu (1883-1935) (Fig. 1-4) formed the distinctive characteristics of what is now known as Yang style *Tai Chi*.

Concerning *Chi Kung, Tai Chi* has two aspects. One is moving meditation which consists of 72 to 128 martial forms (depending on the style and manner of counting) which are practiced in slow motion. During the practice, the body is relaxed, and the *Chi* generated at the *Dan Tien* is continuously guided by the will to circulate throughout the whole body. The other part is still meditation. *Tai Chi* meditation is a form of Taoist meditation which will be explained in detail in Chapter 3. Today the best known of the *Tai Chi* styles are the Chen, Yang, and Wu. Each of these styles has subdivisions which emphasize different postures and applications.

Tai Chi Chuan also includes training with sword, saber, spear, and staff to extend the *Chi*.

Fig. 1-5. Tung Hai-Chuan

Fig. 1-6. Tomb of Tung Hai-Chuan in Peking. Rebuilt in 1981

Ba Kua Chuan

Ba Kua Chuan (The Eight Trigrams Fist), also known as *Ba Kua Chang* (The Eight Trigrams Palm) has a short history. It was created in Peking by Tung Hai-Chuan (Figs. 1-5 and 1-6), a native of Wen An district of Hebei province sometime between 1866 and 1880 A.D. According to several historical records,

Tung learned his martial arts in Giou Hwa Mountain from Bi Dern-Shai. The style is a combination of the best features of the Shaolin (Buddhist) and *Wu Dan* (Taoist) martial arts. *Ba Kua* emphasizes the application of palm techniques and circular movements. It lays stress on the stability and consolidation of the stance and the flexibility of the waist, which is complimented by the swiftness of the arms and palms. When practicing, the devotee's mind controls the waist, and the waist controls the movement of the body in coordination with circular walking around an imagined center point. The movements of the three levels (low, center, and high) result in increasing the practitioner's coordination, strength, and vigor.

The system includes two sets of palm techniques, *Yin* and *Yang*. The highest level of *Ba Kua* practice is called the Dragon Form. In this form the student moves not only in a circle around an imaginary center, but also rotates, twisting and turning, wheeling and moving vertically in combinations. The circular movements of *Ba Kua* are different from the straight line attack of *Hsing Yi*, but its fast motion and internal power training are the same, although both are different from *Tai Chi* and *Liu Ho Pa Fa*.

Hsing Yi

Hsing Yi consists of a set of fast punching movements. There are five basic punches based on the five basic motions: expand, contract, rise, fall and cross. They are performed with the muscles relaxed, however, and the practitioner usually steps in a straight line while punching. In Chinese *Hsing* means "shape" and *Yi* means "mind", so that *Hsing Yi* means "using the mind to determine the form". Marshal Yeuh Fei (1103-1141 A.D.) is popularly credited with creating *Hsing Yi*, although there is no documentary evidence to support the claim. It was not until the end of the Ming dynasty (1644 A.D.) that the documentary history of *Hsing Yi* began. A martial artist named Gi Long-Fon of Shanxi province claimed to have obtained a book, *Chuan Ching* or Fist Fighting Classic, written by Yeuh Fei when he visited a hermit on Tsong Nan Mountain. The book described martial techniques imitating the dragon, tiger, monkey, horse, camel, rooster, eagle, bear, snake, hawk, and swallow. After studying this book, Gi used his knowledge to develop the art and make a more complete style. In the three hundred years since then, other styles of *Hsing Yi* have been developed and practiced. *Hsing Yi* masters were frequently employed as caravan guards beginning in the 19th century. Today there are ten styles of *Hsing Yi* popularly practiced: *Wu Hsing Chuan, Shih Da Hsing, Shih Er Hsing, Pa Shih, Gar Shih Chuan, Shih Er Hen Chuan, Chu Zu Don, An Shen Pou, Giau Shan Pou,* and *Wu Fa Pou.*

Hsing Yi is practiced at a fast speed, although with the muscles relaxed, and power is developed and concentrated in the *Dan Tien*. This is different from *Tai Chi* in which slow motion is practiced at first.

Liu Ho Pa Fa

According to tradition, *Liu Ho Pa Fa* was created during the Sung dynasty (960-1279 A.D.) by Chen Bou, a hermit living on Hua Shan (Mt. Hua). Although it is quite different from *Tai Chi*, it has a common principle that blunt force is forbidden. Both styles emphasize the principle of continuity and the alternate application of soft and hard hand techniques. *Liu Ho Pa Fa* uses *Liu Ho* (the six combinations) as its theory and *Pa Fa* (the eight methods) as its practice. The Six Combinations are:

1. The body combines and coordinates with the mind.
2. The mind combines and coordinates with the idea.
3. The idea combines and coordinates with the *Chi*.
4. The *Chi* combines and coordinates with the spirit.
5. The spirit combines and coordinates with the movements.
6. The movements combine and coordinate with the universe.

These six combinations are achieved by means of the eight methods:

1. *Chi* (Breath)-controlling breathing through concentration.
2. *Ku* (Bone)-Mustering force within the bones.
3. *Hsing* (Shape)-Imitating the various forms and postures.
4. *Hsui* (Following)-Fluidly combining with the opponent's moves.
5. *Ti* (Lift)-Feeling that one is suspended by the top of the head.
6. *Huan* (Return)-Balancing your motion and posture.
7. *Le* (Reserve)-Maintaining peace and calmness of mind.
8. *Fu* (Conceal)-Refraining from exposing one's intentions prematurely.

CHAPTER 2
WAI DAN

2-1. Introduction

Wai Dan (pronounced "Why Don") is the practice of increasing *Chi* circulation by stimulating one area of the body until a large energy potential builds up and overflows through the *Chi* channel system. In Chinese the term *Wai Dan* also signifies the alchemical elixir of life (also called *Gin Dan*), and it is probable that our use of the term derives from the alchemical usage. Most Chinese alchemical texts are products of the Taoists, who were a significant force in the development of *Chi Kung*, so it seems natural to call these Chi Kung training techniques which promote health, strength, and longevity by the Taoist name.

In this chapter the principles of *Wai Dan Chi Kung* practice will be explained first. Then the most famous Shaolin *Wai Dan* training method, Da Mo's *Yi Gin Ching* will be introduced. Next a number of other sets of *Wai Dan* training will be shown, including the well known set, Eight Pieces of Brocade (*Ba Dun Gin*). The reader should try all the exercises presented, then adopt a training schedule suited to his own needs. You can pick one set and practice that every day for several months or years, or do a different set every day. The needs of the student will change as he develops, so one should maintain a flexible attitude toward the training.

2-2. Theory of Wai Dan

There are two types of *Wai Dan* exercise, moving and still. In moving *Wai Dan*, a specific muscle or part of the body is repeatedly tensed and relaxed with full attention. The tension should be as little as possible because great tension will constrict the channels and prevent the flow of energy. Some people do not tense their muscles at all, but merely imagine tensing them. Others tense them just enough to aid concentration. When one exercises a part of the body in this way for several minutes, the *Chi* accumulates in that area, which usually results in a local feeling of warmth. At this time not only the energy, but also the blood will be collected in this high potential area. When the muscles relax, the highly charged *Chi* and blood will spread to nearby low energy areas and so increase the *Chi* circulation.

According to acupuncture theory the *Chi* channels are connected to the internal organs. If *Chi* is circulating smoothly, then the organs will function normally. If an organ is not functioning normally, then increasing the *Chi* flow in the corresponding channel will help to restore its normal function.

In moving *Wai Dan* exercises the mind concentrates on the breath and at the same time imagines guiding energy to the local area. As was mentioned earlier, the channel system and the brain are closely related, so that when one concentrates, he can control the circulation of *Chi* more efficiently. This in turn results in the muscles being able to exert maximum power. This is what is known as *Wai Dan* internal power. For example in order to guide the *Chi* you have generated to the center of the palm, imagine an obstacle in front of your palm and try to push it away without tensing any muscles. The better you imagine, the stronger the *Chi* flow will be. Frequently, when an object seems too heavy to move, and you have tried in vain to push it, if you relax and calm down and imagine pushing the object, you will find the object will now move. Therefore, in practicing the moving *Wai Dan* exercises, you should be calm, relaxed and natural. The muscles should never be strongly tensed, because this tension will narrow the *Chi* channels. The mind should be concentrated on breathing with the *Dan Tien* and on guiding the *Chi*.

There is a disadvantage of *Wai Dan* moving exercises, however. Because of the repeated tensing and relaxing of the muscles during training, the muscle itself will be built up, as in weight lifting, and can become overdeveloped. This overdevelopment will slow you down, and at the same time will constrict the channels. When these overdeveloped muscles are not regularly exercised, they accumulate fat, which will further narrow the channels and the *Chi* and blood will become stagnant. Common symptoms of this phenomenon are high blood pressure, local nerve pain, and poor muscle control. In the Chinese martial arts this is called "*San Kung*" or "Energy Dispersion". As long as the practitioner avoids overdeveloping his muscles, *San Kung* will not happen.

In still *Wai Dan* specific muscle groups are also stressed, although they are not tensed. For example, one type of still *Wai Dan* is practiced by extending both arms level in front of the body and holding the posture. After several minutes the nerves in the arms and shoulder area become excited to a higher energy state, and when you drop your arms and relax, the generated *Chi* will circulate to areas of lower potential, much like an electric battery circulates electricity when a circuit is made. Because the muscle is not being exercised, there is no danger here of overdevelopment, as there is in the case of moving *Wai Dan*, so consequently there is no risk of *San Kung*. Although the muscle is not built up in still *Wai Dan*, its endurance is increased. Still *Wai Dan* exercises, however, are only effective for promoting health, not for use in the martial arts. This is because they do not train the coordination of energy circulation with muscular exertion.

If a practitioner of *Wai Dan* also has training in *Nei Dan*, he can accumulate *Chi* in the *Dan Tien* with breathing and concentration and guide this energy to the area being stressed to enhance the *Chi* circulation. In this case the method is a mixture of *Wai Dan* and *Nei Dan*, and this kind of training is commonly used in the practice of *Tai Chi Chuan*.

2-3. Da Mo's "Yi Gin Ching"

Da Mo (Fig. 2-1), whose last name was Sardili, and who was also known as Bodhidarma, was a prince of a small tribe in southern India. From the fragments of historical records that exist it is believed he was born about 483 A.D. At that time India was considered a spiritual center by the Chinese, since

像法師祖摩達

Fig. 2-1. Da Mo

it was the source of Buddhism, which was becoming very influential in China. Many of the Chinese emperors either sent priests to India to study Buddhism and bring back scriptures, or else they invited Indian priests to come to China to preach. Da Mo was one of the latter.

He is considered by many to have been a *bodhisattva*, or an enlightened being who had renounced *nirvana* in order to save others. Briefly, Buddhism is a major religion based on the belief that Gautama, the Buddha, achieved *nirvana*, or perfect bliss and freedom from the cycle of birth and death, and taught how to achieve this state. Buddhists have divided into three principal groups

Fig. 2-2. Shaolin Temple

practicing different versions of the Buddha's teaching, which are called the "three conveyances" or "Shan Sheng". The first of these is *Mahayana* or "*Da Sheng*", the Great Vehicle, which includes Tibetan Buddhism and *Chan* or *Zen* Buddhism which is very well known to the west. The second is *Praktika* or "*Chung Sheng*", the Middle Way, which is the Buddhism of action, and is mostly practiced by wandering preachers. The third is *Hinayana* or "*Shao Sheng*", the Lesser Conveyance, which is generally practiced by ascetic monks and aims at personal achievement of enlightenment.

Da Mo was of the *Mahayana* school and came to China in 526 or 527 A.D. during the reign of Emperor Liang Wu of the Liang dynasty. He went first to the Kuan Shao Temple in Canton. The governor of Canton, Shaou Yon recommended Da Mo to the emperor, who invited Da Mo to visit. The emperor, however, did not like Da Mo's Buddhist theory, and so Da Mo traveled to the Shaolin Temple (Fig. 2-2) in Henan province where he spent the rest of his life.

The Shaolin Temple was built in 377 A.D. on the Shao Shih peak of Sonn Mountain in Teng Fon Hsien, Henan province, by order of Emperor Wei for

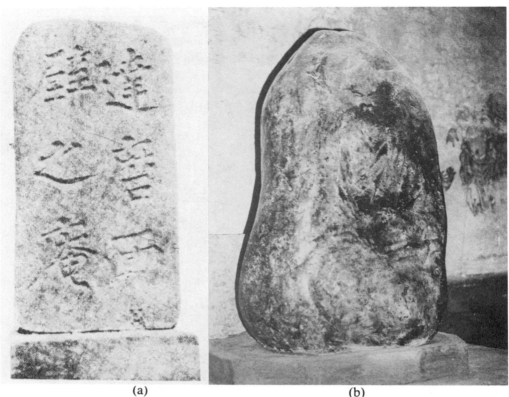

Fig. 2-3. (a) A Stone Monument at the place where Da Mo
faced a stone wall in meditation

(b) A rock with Da Mo's image found at the place where he meditated

a Buddhist named Pao Jaco for the purpose of preaching and worship. In the
beginning no martial arts training was done by the monks.

When Da Mo arrived at the temple, he saw that the monks were generally
in poor physical condition because of their lack of exercise. He was so distress-
ed by the situation that he retired to meditate on the problem, and stayed in
retirement for nine years (Fig. 2-3). During that time he wrote two books, but
only one, the *Yi Gin Ching* (Book of Muscle Development), survives. After he
came out of retirement, Da Mo continued to live in the Shaolin Temple until
his death in 540 A.D. at the age of 57.

Lu Yu, a poet of the Southern Sung dynasty (1131-1162 A.D.), wrote a poem
(see Appendix for Chinese) describing Da Mo's personal philosophy:

Others are revolted, I am unmoved

Gripped by desires, I am unmoved

Hearing the wisdom of sages, I am unmoved

I move only in my own way.

For more than 1400 years the monks of the Shaolin Temple have trained using the Da Mo *Wai Dan* exercises. These exercises used to be secret and they
have only started to become popularly known and used by the Chinese people
in the twentieth century. These exercises are easy and their benefits are experienced in a short time. The Shaolin monks practice these exercises not just to circulate *Chi* and improve their health, but also to build their interal power by
concentrating *Chi* to affect the appropriate muscles. Because these exercises are

moving *Wai Dan*, there is the risk of *San Kung* or Energy Dispersion, as mentioned earlier. To avoid *San Kung*, the monks also practiced *Nei Dan* meditation to keep their channels clear after they quit the Da Mo exercises.

The practitioner should find a place with clean air and stand facing the east with the back relaxed and naturally straight, the feet shoulder width apart and parallel. Facing the east takes advantage of the earth's rotation and the energy flow from the sun. Keeping the legs apart will relax the legs and thighs during the practice. Keep the mouth closed and touch the palate with the tip of the tongue without strain. In Chinese meditation this touch is call "*Da Chiao*" or "Building the Bridge" because it connects the *Yin* and *Yang* circulation (a detailed explanation of this will follow in Chapter 3, *Nei Dan*). The practitioner will find that saliva accumulates in the mouth. This should be swallowed to keep the throat from getting dry from the concentration on breathing.

The concentration of the mind on the area being exercised and on the breath is the key to successful practice of this exercise. Without this concentration the original goal of *Chi* circulation will be lost and the exercise will be in vain.

There are several circumstances when practice should be avoided. First, when one is very hungry or too full. If you are very hungry it interferes with proper concentration. Wait at least 30 minutes and preferably one hour after eating so that the *Chi* is not so concentrated in the digestive system. Second, avoid practicing one day before or after having sex. Third, do not practice when you are so tired that your attention wanders uncontrollably. Fourth, do not practice after drinking alcohol. And finally, do not practice when you are very worried, for it will be too difficult to concentrate.

The forms should be done one after the other continuously in order to conserve the energy built up. For example, the first form will build up the energy at the wrist. The second will transfer the energy already built up at the wrist to the fingers and palm, and continue to build up energy. The third form will transfer the energy from the palm and wrist to the arm, and so forth.

Practice each form 50 times. A repetition consists of inhaling while relaxing the muscle or limb and exhaling while imagining that you are tightening the muscle and imagining energy flowing to that area. The muscles may be slightly tensed. The arms should not be fully extended in these forms. After 50 repetitions begin the next form in the sequence without stopping. Beginners will find it hard to complete more than five forms in one practice session, and five forms is a good number to practice anyway, since this means a session of 15 to 20 minutes. Alternatively, the practitioner can practice the entire 12 forms with fewer repetitions of each one, so that with twenty repetitions each, the form would again take about twenty minutes. If you practice once or twice a day, you should be able to complete the entire form in six months. If you continue this training for three years, a tremendous amount of power and energy can be built up. These exercises will increase the nerve and muscle efficiency so they can be used to their maximum in martial arts. For health purposes, practicing five forms daily should be enough.

Fig. 2-4.   Fig. 2-5.   Fig. 2-6.

Da Mo Wai Dan

The Da Mo set consists of twelve forms:

Form 1 (Fig. 2-4):

Hold the hands beside the body with the palms open and facing down, fingertips pointing forward. Keep the elbows bent. Imagine pushing the palms down when exhaling and relax them when inhaling. This form will build the *Chi* or energy at the wrist area, and the palm and wrist should feel warm after 50 repetitions.

Form 2 (Fig. 2-5):

Without moving the arms make fists with palms facing down and thumbs extended toward the body. Imagine tightening the fists and pushing the thumbs backwards when exhaling, relax when inhaling. The wrists are kept bent backward to retain the energy built up in the first form.

Form 3 (Fig. 2-6):

Again without moving the arms turn the fists so that the palms face each other and place the thumbs over the fingers, like a normal fist. Imagine tightening the fists when exhaling, relax when inhaling. The muscles and nerves of the arms will be stimulated and energy will accumulate there.

Form 4 (Fig. 2-7):

Extend the arms straight in front of the body, palms still facing each other. Making normal fists, imagine tightening when exhaling; relax when inhaling. This will build up energy in the shoulders and chest.

Form 5 (Fig. 2-8):

Extend the arms straight up, palms facing each other, keeping the fists. Imagine tightening the fists when exhaling; relax when inhaling. This builds energy in the shoulders, neck and sides.

Fig. 2-7.

Fig. 2-8.

Fig. 2-9.

Fig. 2-10.

Fig. 2-11.

Fig. 2-12.

Form 6 (Fig. 2-9):

Lower the arms so that the upper arms are parallel with the ground, the elbows bent and the fists by the ears palms forward. Imagine tightening the fists when exhaling, relax when inhaling. This builds energy in the sides, chest, and upper arms.

Form 7 (Fig. 2-10):

Extend the arms straight out to the sides with the palms facing forward. Imagine tightening the fists when exhaling; relax when inhaling. This form will build energy in the shoulders, chest, and back.

Form 8 (Fig. 2-11):

Extend the arms straight in front of the body with the palms facing each other, but with the elbows bent slightly to create a rounded effect with the arms. Imagine tightening the fists and guiding the accumulated energy through the arms to the fists when exhaling; relax when inhaling.

Fig. 2-13.   Fig. 2-14.   Fig. 2-15.

Form 9 (Fig. 2-12):

Pull the fists toward the body, bending the elbows. Fists are just in front of the face, palms forward. Imagine tightening the fists when exhaling; relax when inhaling. This form is similar to 6 above, but the fists are closer together and forward, so a different set of muscles is stressed. It intensifies the flow of energy through the arms.

Form 10 (Fig.2-13):

Raise the forearms vertically. Fists face forward, upper arms out to the side and parallel with the floor. Imagine tightening the fists when exhaling, relax when inhaling. This form will circulate the energy built up in the shoulder area.

Form 11 (Fig.2-14):

Keeping the elbows bent, lower the fists until they are in front of the lower abdomen, palms down. Imagine tightening the fists and guide the energy to circulate in the arms when exhaling, relax when inhaling. This is the first recovery form.

Form 12 (Fig.2-15):

Raise the arms straight out in front of the body, palms open, facing up. Imagine lifting up when exhaling, relax when inhaling. This is the second recovery form.

After practicing, stand awhile with the arms hanging loosely at the sides, or better, lie down and relax completely. Breathe regularly, relax, and feel the energy redistribute itself for a few minutes.

2-4.   Other Wai Dan Exercises

There are many other sets of *Wai Dan* exercises which are derived from Da Mo's sequence. In this section the most common *Wai Dan* sets will be introduced. These are the Open Palm Sequence, which moves power to the fingertips; Moving Forms for coordinating breathing with movement of the arms, legs, and trunk; and Eight Pieces of Brocade, a set of simple exercises well known throughout China. In addition a set of Still Forms which can be used to develop stamina and flexibility will be included.

Open Palm Sequence

The open palm forms give training in extending energy to the palms and fingertips. In this set the hands should be kept relaxed, except that the thumbs and little fingers are pulled back and tightened slightly so that energy is directed to the centers of the palms. To understand how to do this, imagine holding a basketball or large balloon in both hands without the thumbs or little fingers touching it.

This set of exercises has the same purpose as the Da Mo *Wai Dan*, so in practicing the same rules and principles should be followed with one difference. Instead of tensing the fist the palm is tensed and the energy is guided to the fingertips continuously.

Fig. 2-16. Fig. 2-17. Fig. 2-18.

Form 1 (Fig. 2-16):
Palms face the floor, while the fingers point out to the sides. Imagine pushing down when exhaling, relax when inhaling.

Form 2 (Fig. 2-17):
Palms face the body, fingers pointing down. Imagine pushing in when exhaling, relax when inhaling.

Form 3 (Fig. 2-18):
Arms are extended out to the sides, palms facing up. Imagine pushing up when exhaling, relax when inhaling.

Form 4 (Fig. 2-19):
Bend the arms and place the hands in front of the chest, palms facing each other, fingers pointing up. Imagine pushing the hands toward each other when exhaling, relax when inhaling.

Fig. 2-19.   Fig. 2-20.   Fig. 2-21.

Fig. 2-22.   Fig. 2-23.   Fig. 2-24.

Form 5 (Fig. 2-20):

Extend the arms out to the sides, palms facing out, fingers pointing up. Imagine pushing out when exhaling, relax when inhaling.

Form 6 (Fig. 2-21):

Bend the arms and place the hands in front of the chest again, with palms touching this time, fingers pointing up. Imagine pushing in when exhaling, relax when inhaling.

Form 7 (Fig. 2-22):

Extend the arms straight out in front, palms facing the front, fingers pointing up. Imagine pushing forward when exhaling, relax when inhaling.

Form 8 (Fig. 2-23):

Extend the arms straight up, palms facing up, fingers pointing toward each other. Imagine pushing up when exhaling, relax when inhaling.

Form 9 (Fig. 2-24):

Lower the hands to the front of the chest, elbows bent, palms facing up, fingers pointing toward each other. Imagine lifting up when exhaling, relax when inhaling.

Fig. 2-25.   Fig. 2-26.   Fig. 2-27.

Form 10 (Fig.2-25):

Extend the arms straight to the front, palms facing up, fingers pointing forward. Imagine pushing up when exhaling, relax when inhaling.

Form 11 (Fig.2-26):

Bring the hands back to the front of the chest, palms facing down, fingers in line. Imagine pushing down when exhaling, relax when inhaling.

Form 12 (Fig.2-27):

Extend the arms out to the side with the elbows bent, palms facing up and a little inward. Imagine lifting upward and inward when exhaling, relax when inhaling.

Just as with the Da Mo *Wai Dan*, after practicing stand awhile with the arms hanging loosely at the sides, or better, lie down and relax completely. Breathe regularly, relax, and feel the energy redistribute itself for a few minutes.

Moving Forms

The Moving Forms give training in large muscle coordination, develop the large muscles, and loosen the joints, particularly the back. These forms are a new development in *Chi Kung* and were created because people felt that the *Yi Gin Ching* forms emphasized the arms to the exclusion of the rest of the body.

When practicing, repeat each form five to ten times:

Fig. 2-28.   Fig. 2-29.   Fig. 2-30.

Fig. 2-31.   Fig. 2-32.   Fig. 2-33.

Form 1 (Figs. 2-28 and 2-29):

Stand erect with the arms at the sides and the feet shoulder width apart. Bend forward and touch the fingertips to the floor, keeping the knees locked straight if possible, then return to a standing posture. Exhale when bending forward, inhale while standing back up.

Form 2 (Figs. 2-30 and 2-31):

Stand erect and hold the palms in front of the chest, facing each other. While exhaling, bring the hands together until they almost touch. When you inhale let the hands separate. While pressing imagine energy flowing to the palms, completing a circuit.

Form 3 (Figs. 2-32 and 2-33):

While exhaling push straight up over your head with one palm while pushing down behind your back with the other. Relax and inhale while reversing the position of the hands.

Fig. 2-34.

Fig. 2-35.

Fig. 2-36.

Fig. 2-37.

Fig. 2-38.

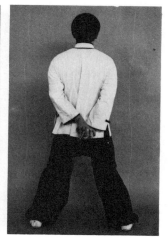
Fig. 2-39.

Form 4 (Figs. 2-34 and 2-35):

Clasp your hands behind your back. Expand the chest when inhaling and relax while exhaling.

Form 5 (Figs. 2-36 and 2-37):

Stand erect with arms hanging at the sides. Rotate the shoulders together 10 times in one direction, 10 times in the other, coordinating with the breathing. It does not matter whether you inhale as the shoulders are moving forward or backward as long as you are consistent.

Form 6 (Fig. 2-38):

Reach behind your back with the left hand and reach over your shoulder with the right hand and clasp hands. Expand the chest while inhaling, and relax when exhaling. Do this 10 times, then reverse the position of the arms and do 10 more times.

Fig. 2-40.   Fig. 2-41.   Fig. 2-42.

Fig. 2-43.   Fig. 2-44.   Fig. 2-45.

Form 7 (Figs. 2-39, 2-40 and 2-41):
 Clasp the hands behind the back while standing in a half squat and
rotate the body from side to side. Exhale while turning to the side and inhale
while facing forward.

Form 8 (Figs. 2-42 and 2-43):
Stand in a half squat with the arms out to the sides, elbows bent. While inhaling turn the palms up and lift up, and while exhaling turn the palms down and
push down.

Form 9 (Figs. 2-44 and 2-45):
Bend forward. When inhaling touch the backs of the hands to the floor in front
of you, and when exhaling remain bent over and press down with the palms
on the back of the neck.

Fig. 2-46.   Fig. 2-47.   Fig. 2-48.

Fig. 2-49.   Fig. 2-50.   Fig. 2-51.

Form 10 (Figs. 2-46 through 2-49):
Stand erect with the arms extended straight in front, palms up. When exhaling, turn the palms down and lower the body by bending your knees, and when inhaling turn the palms up and stand back up.

Form 11 (Figs. 2-50 and 2-51):
Stand with the feet as far apart as comfortable. Shift most of the weight to the right foot and at the same time turn to the right, raising the right arm diagonally upward, palm facing out and up, and pointing the fingers of the left hand in the opposite direction. Think of the two arms as one unit forming a straight line. Then reverse, shifting most of the weight to the left foot and at the same time turning to the left, raising the left arm diagonally upward, palm facing out and up, and pointing the fingers of the right hand in the opposite direction. Exhale while stretching, and inhale while changing sides.

Fig. 2-52.   Fig. 2-53.

Form 12 (Figs. 2-52 and 2-53):
Stand with the feet as far apart as is comfortable. Shift most of the weight to the left foot and at the same time turn to the left, bending the body sideways with the right arm in front of the head, and the left arm behind the back, both palms facing out. Twist to the left as far as possible with the feeling of spiral-ling, or pushing, through both hands. Then reverse, shifting most of the weight to the right foot and at the same time turning to the right, reversing the arms. Exhale while stretching, and inhale while changing sides.

Eight Pieces of Brocade

Marshal Yueh Fei is credited with the creation of the Eight Pieces of Brocade *(Ba Dun Gin)* in the twelfth century during the Sung dynasty (960-1279 A.D.) in order to improve the health of his soldiers. The original set consisted of 12 forms, but this has been shortened to eight.

This set was widely practiced all over China, and developed several distinct styles, all of them effective. The brocade is a cloth, usually of silk, woven into complex and colorful patterns, and is very highly prized, just as the good health produced by these simple exercises is highly prized.

When performing the set, the following rules should be observed:

Relax before and after exercising, perhaps by taking a short walk.
Breathe naturally through the nose.
Keep the back vertical, except where leaning is part of the exercise.
Practice where ventilation is good.
Perform the exercises slowly and keep relaxed.
Repeat each piece three to five times.
Perform the movements one after the other without stopping until a complete set is done, then repeat the complete set as many times as desired.

Fig. 2-54.   Fig. 2-55.   Fig. 2-56.

Fig. 2-57.   Fig. 2-58.

Piece 1 (Figs. 2-54 through 2-58):

Stand with the feet parallel and shoulder width apart. Inahle. While exhaling turn the head as far to the left as possible without moving the rest of the body and look to the rear. While inhaling return the gaze to the front. Exhale while turning the head as far as possible to the right and looking to the rear, then inhale while looking to the front again.

Piece 2 (Figs. 2-59 through 2-63):

Lace the fingers together in front of the body with the palms facing up. While exhaling, swing the arms out in front of the chest and then up until the arms are overhead with the palms facing up. Inhale while returning the hands to their starting position.

Fig. 2-59.   Fig. 2-60.   Fig. 2-61.

Fig. 2-62.   Fig. 2-63.

Piece 3 (Figs. 2-64 through 2-68):

Hold the hands in front of the body with hands facing up and the middle fingers pointing toward each other. While exhaling, simultaneously move the left hand overhead palm up and the right hand down palm down. While inhaling bring the hands to their original position. While exhaling simultaneously raise the right hand overhead palm up and move the left hand down palm down. Inhale and return to the original position.

Piece 4 (Figs. 2-69 through 2-79):

Make fists at the sides, palms up. While inhaling step to the left and assume a horse stance. While exhaling turn the body slightly to the left and cross the arms in front of the chest. Curl the three small fingers of the left hand and make a "V" with the index finger and the thumb. Look at the index finger and extend it horizontally to the left while exhaling. At the same time make

Fig. 2-64.

Fig. 2-65.

Fig. 2-66.

Fig. 2-67.

Fig. 2-68.

Fig. 2-69.

Fig. 2-70.

Fig. 2-71.

Fig. 2-72.   Fig. 2-73.   Fig. 2-74.

Fig. 2-75.   Fig. 2-76.   Fig. 2-77.

Fig. 2-78.   Fig. 2-79.

a fist with the right hand and pull it back to the right shoulder, much like drawing a bow. While inhaling bring the fists back to the sides and return to the starting position. Repeat the exercise for the right side.

Piece 5 (Figs. 2-80 through 2-84):

Step to the left and assume the horse stance. Place the palms on the thighs near the knees with the fingers inward. Lean as far to the left as possible without raising the feet, and keep the hands on the thighs. Lean to the right.

Piece 6 (Figs. 2-85 through 2-87):

Bring the feet back to shoulder width. Hold the hands in front of the body with the palms facing up and the middle fingers pointing toward each other. Straighten the legs and lock the knees, then while exhaling bend forward and touch the floor with the palms, keeping the legs straight. Do not strain.

Fig. 2-80.   Fig. 2-81.   Fig. 2-82.

Fig. 2-83.   Fig. 2-84.

Fig. 2-85.

Fig. 2-86.

Fig. 2-87.

Fig. 2-88.

Fig. 2-89.

Fig. 2-90.

Stretch up to but not beyond the point of pain. Return to the original position while inhaling.

Piece 7 (Figs. 2-88 through 2-92):
Stand in a horse stance with the fists at the sides. While exhaling, slowly strike upward and to the left with the left fist. Keep the gaze on the fist throughout. Return to the starting position while inhaling and do the movement with the right fist.

Piece 8 (Figs. 2-93 through 2-95):
Stand with the feet close together and the arms hanging loosely by the sides. Stretch the legs and lock the knees, then raise the heels as high as possible while exhaling, then let yourself down while inhaling.

Fig. 2-91.   Fig. 2-92.

Fig. 2-93.   Fig. 2-94.   Fig. 2-95.

Still Wai Dan Forms

Some of the still forms are very similar to Indian Yoga, which is not surprising, since China looked to India as a spiritual source for many years. The forms should be performed in as relaxed a manner as possible, tensing only the muscles needed to do the posture. Place the tip of the tongue against the roof of the mouth and breathe deeply from the lower abdomen.

Form 1 (Fig. 2-96):

Lie on your back with the legs together and the arms at your sides. Keeping the legs straight, raise the feet about a foot off the floor, and at the same time raise the upper torso a similar distance. Breathe deeply and hold the position for 30 seconds to two minutes.

Fig. 2-96.

Fig. 2-97.

Form 2 (Fig. 2-97):

Stretch out with the head on one chair and the feet on another with the body straight and hold from 30 seconds to two minutes. As one might guess this posture is very difficult. It is almost essential to do self-hypnosis to practice it. This is the advanced form of Form 1. In Chinese martial arts training this form is called "Iron Board Bridge" *(Tiea Bann Chiao)*.

Form 3 (Figs. 2-98 and 2-99):

Lie on the floor on your stomach. Bend the knees and reach back and grasp the ankles or feet. Pull the feet and head toward each other on inhalation and relax on exhalation.

Form 4 (Figs. 2-100 and 2-101):

Lie on the floor on your stomach with the arms stretched forward. Lift the upper body and the feet off the floor simultaneously when inhaling, relax when exhaling. In Yoga this form is called the locust.

Form 5 (Figs. 2-102 and 2-103):

Lie on the floor and grasp your feet. Slowly straighten the legs while exhaling. Bend the legs into the original position while inhaling.

Form 6 (Fig. 2-104):

Lie on your back with the arms by your side. Raise the legs to vertical, then continue to lift, raising the buttocks and torso off the floor. If your balance is unsteady, you may bend your elbows and use the hands to support the trunk in a vertical position. The weight is on the shoulders and the upper arms, not on the neck. Hold this position for at least one minute breathing slowly and deeply. This is known as the shoulder stand.

Fig. 2-98.

Fig. 2-99.

Fig. 2-100.

Fig. 2-101.

Fig. 2-102.

Fig. 2-103.

Fig. 2-104.

Fig. 2-105.

Fig. 2-106.

Fig. 2-107.

Form 7 (Figs. 2-105 and 2-106):

Lie on your right side, left knee bent so that your left knee and lower leg rest on the floor. The right arm is straight out in front of you, left arm is along your side. While inhaling, turn your torso so that your left shoulder and upper arm touch the floor. Your left leg remains in position. While exhaling, roll back to the starting position on the right side. Do this 25 times, then switch sides and repeat 25 times.

Form 8 (Fig. 2-107)

Assume the pushup position, resting the weight on the fingertips, keeping the back straight. Hold 30 seconds to one minute.

Form 9 (Figs. 2-108 and 2-109):

This posture is called "The Child Worships the Buddha" *(Ton Tzu Bai For)*. Stand on one leg and extend the other straight out in front, parallel with the floor. Press the palms together in front of the chest. Hold 30 seconds on each leg. As an advanced technique, bend the knee and lower the body on inhalation, stand back up on exhalation.

Form 10 (Fig. 2-110):

Stand on one leg in a half squat with the palms pressed together in front of the chest again, but this time the free leg is held out in front of the body. Hold for up to three minutes on each leg.

Fig. 2-108.   Fig. 2-109.

Fig. 2-110.   Fig. 2-111.   Fig. 2-112.

Form 11 (Fig. 2-111):

Stand in a half squat with the feet shoulder width apart and parallel. Raise the arms up until the palms face the ceiling. Bend the head back and look straight up. Hold one to three minutes. This is called *"Tou Tian"* (or Holding up the Sky).

Form 12 (Fig. 2-112):

Stand on one leg with the free toe just touching the floor in front of the body. Raise the arms to a horizontal circle in front of the chest, palms facing in. Hold three minutes for each leg.

The main purpose of this chapter has been to introduce the principles and theory of *Wai Dan* exercises. Although several sets of traditional *Wai Dan* forms have been presented, the reader should be able to create his own forms as long as he understands the theory thoroughly. The new forms should generate the sensation of *Chi* flow in the areas or sets of muscles being exercised.

CHAPTER 3
NEI DAN

3-1. Introduction

Nei Dan (pronounced "Nay Don") literally means "internal elixir". It is a training method in which the *Chi* is generated in the abdomen and then guided by the mind throughout the body. As was explained in Chapter 1, when the muscles are exercised, *Chi* and blood will accumulate in the area of the body being exercised. When the muscle is then relaxed the channels open wide and allow the accumulated energy to flow from the area that was exercised and circulate throughout the body. This exercising with exterior muscles, called *Wai Dan*, was discussed in the previous chapter. The results are different when this kind of exercise is done while focusing on the lower abdomen, the *Dan Tien* or *Qihai* area, as is done in *Nei Dan*. The energy built up in the lower abdomen can be guided by the will to circulate around the body through the two major vessels, the Governing (*Du Mei*) and Conception (*Ren Mei*) Vessels, which are centered in the back and front of the torso. This is called the "Small Circulation" (*Shao Chou Tien*). Eventually this energy can be directed throughout the body through all the twelve *Chi* channels; this is called the "Grand Circulation" (*Da Chou Tien*).

The history of *Nei Dan* can be traced back to the very beginning of *Chi Kung* practice in China. Originally, judging from the record of Buddhist and Taoist scriptures, it was used to promote physical and spiritual health, as it still is now. The people who learned meditation were scholars, Buddhist and Taoist monks, and a few of the common people, often sick people, trying to regain their health.

In the thirteenth century a Taoist martial style was created which specialized in using the internal power created with *Nei Dan*. Though the breathing techniques used for training are different from those of the Buddhists, the principles are the same. Chang San-Feng (Fig. 3-1) is credited with creating the style now known as *Tai Chi Chuan* in the Wu Dan Mountain area (Fig. 3-2) located to the South of Chun Hsien, Hubei Province in China. Since that time several other *Nei Dan* styles based on the Wu Dan principles have been developed such as *Ba Kua*, *Hsing Yi*, and *Liu Ho Ba Fa*.

In the hundreds of years that have passed since then both Shaolin *Kung Fu* and *Tai Chi* have kept their respective emphasis on *Wai Dan* and *Nei Dan*. It was not until the late 19th century and beginning of the 20th century, when both Shaolin *Kung Fu* and *Tai Chi Chuan* were generally exposed to the Chinese

Fig. 3-1. Chang San-Feng

public, that martial artists commonly began to practice both *Nei Dan* and *Wai Dan*.

The reader should understand that there were many other martial and non-martial styles of *Wai Dan* and *Nei Dan* created throughout Chinese history in addition to Shaolin *Kung Fu* and *Tai Chi Chuan* that were popular with the Chinese people. However, most of these styles have died out and the styles mentioned above have dominated the popular interest since the turn of the century.

Also, many of the non-martial systems do not use the *Dan Tien* as the source of *Chi*, but rather use some other point on the Governing or Conception Vessels, such as the solar plexus or the point between the eyebrows. Energy is generated by concentrating on a selected point and not through moving the abdominal muscles. These meditation systems are outside the scope of this book and will not be discussed.

Compared with *Wai Dan*, *Nei Dan* has both advantages and disadvantages. The disadvantages are: first, with *Nei Dan* it takes a longer time to experience the *Chi* in the *Dan Tien* than it does to feel energy in the local area using *Wai Dan*. Therefore, *Wai Dan Chi Kung* can be easily applied in the martial arts in a short time and one can see improved health and power in a limited time. Second, *Nei Dan* training requires instruction from a more qualified master than *Wai Dan*. Usually, *Wai Dan* training is quite straight-forward once the principles and the forms are understood. However, because in *Nei Dan* it is harder to experience *Chi*, the student requires the master's advice and experienced analysis to advance step by step. Third, *Nei Dan* requires more patience and

Fig. 3-2. Wu Dan Mountain

a calmer mind than *Wai Dan*. Fourth, more caution and help from the master is necessary in order to avoid injury. Since *Nei Dan* generates a large amount of *Chi* and starts circulating it in the vital Governing and Conception Vessels, some of the *Chi* can stagnate in the cavities of these vessels. Also, the *Chi* generated can get out of the meditator's control, go into an unexpected channel and stay in the cavities of that channel. This *Chi* residue can be a danger if a practitioner does not know how to handle the problem.

On the other hand *Nei Dan* has several advantages compared with *Wai Dan*. First, *Nei Dan* teaches awareness of *Chi* circulation and develops this circulation more fully throughout the body, which benefits the organs much better than *Wai Dan* does. As the reader already knows, *Wai Dan* circulates the Chi locally and therefore benefits only specific organs. Second, the *Nei Dan* practitioner does not have the risk of *San Kung* or Energy Dispersion, since it does not build up the body's muscles except for those of the lower abdomen (the *Dan Tien* area), and once a person practices *Nei Dan* for a few years, he will naturally use the *Dan Tien* all the time. Third, once the *Nei Dan* circulation is completed, the internal power it can build for martial purposes is much stronger than that of *Wai Dan*.

Very commonly, Chinese martial artists train in both *Wai Dan* and *Nei Dan*, while non-martial artists usually practice only one for health purposes.

Nei Dan can be roughly divided into Buddhist and Taoist styles. The major differences are, first, in training emphasis. Buddhists emphasize raising the *Chi (Yang Chi)*, in which the *Chi* is maintained through calmness and concentrated in the brain in order to reach enlightenment. In China maintaining *Chi* through calmness is called "*Tsao Chan*", or sitting meditation. In Taoist practice, however, the breath at the *Dan Tien* is emphasized to build up the *Chi* and to make it stronger and stronger. This is called "*Lien Chi*" or Strengthening the *Chi*. After the *Chi* is built up, then the Taoist will circulate the *Chi* through the body by guiding it with his will. This is called Transporting the *Chi (Yun Chi)* or Circulating the *Chi (Hsing Chi)*. This kind of Taoist Chi Kung training is commonly called "*Yun Kung*" or "*Hsing Kung*" which means the *Kung Fu* of *Chi* transportation.

Second, in *Chi* training, Buddhists use natural breathing in which the abdomen is sucked in when exhaling and is expanded when inhaling, while the Taoists use the reverse breathing technique in which the abdomen is sucked in when inhaling and expanded when exhaling. This possibly stems from the Taoists using *Nei Dan* in martial applications and finding that it is easier to get the internal power out strongly when the *Dan Tien* is expanded while exhaling and sinking the *Chi*.

In this chapter the next section will explain the principles of *Nei Dan*, and how the *Chi* is generated and circulated. The methods of *Nei Dan* training, both Buddhist and Taoist, will be introduced in section three. In section four, the secret training methods which teach the meditator to strengthen his *Chi* and to guide it to particular areas for martial purposes will be discussed. Finally, exercises and self massage techniques for after meditation will be presented in section five to close this chapter.

3-2. Principles of Nei Dan

As was explained before, the exercise in which *Chi* is generated in the *Dan Tien* or *Qihai* and then guided by the mind to complete the entire body energy circulation is called *Nei Dan*. The location of the Dan Tien is about 1.5 inches directly below the navel and one third of the way through the body. The name *Dan Tien* means "Field of Elixir" and was used by Taoist meditators. The name *Qihai* is used by acupuncturists and means "Sea of *Chi*". The *Dan Tien* is considered to be the original source of a person's energy, because the embryo uses the lower abdomen to circulate its supply of nourishment and oxygen from its mother. After the baby is born, it continues to breathe with emphasis on the lower belly for several years, gradually moving the focus of breathing higher and higher in the torso, so that by late childhood, people think of themselves as breathing with their chests, and in fact they have lost control of their lower abdominal muscles. In *Nei Dan* meditation the practitioner returns to the embryonic method of breathing; at least the focus of breathing returns to the *Dan Tien* because it is considered the source of *Chi* circulation. The *Dan Tien* is also called the furnace or "*For Lu*" (relating meditation to Taoism's alchemical tradition) in which the fire or energy can be started.

An important Taoist book is *Tai Shih Ching* or Classic of Harmonized Embryonic Breathing (see Appendix A for Chinese version). It emphasizes the importance of the *Dan Tien* and regulated breathing, and recommends the nurturing of the *Dan Tien* as if it were an embryo. This idea is sometimes portrayed in Taoist art by a person meditating with a baby over his head.

Principles From The Tai Shih Ching
The embryo is generated from the hidden or undeveloped *Chi*.
Chi comes from the modulated breathing of the embryo.
When *Chi* enters the body-life. When Spirit leaves the body and the embryo disperses-death.
Knowing Spirit and *Chi* makes a long life possible. Protect and nourish the imaginary embryo to build up Spirit and *Chi*.
When Spirit moves, the *Chi* moves; where Spirit stops, the *Chi* stops.
To have a long life, Spirit and *Chi* must mutually interact.
When the heart (mind) is not dispersed, not a thought goes or comes.
When thoughts are not going and coming, nature is.
The true way to approach this goal is through hard work.

Over thousands of years of experience, Chinese meditators found that through practice they could retrain the abdominal muscles and regain a stronger flow of *Chi*. This exercise is called "Back to Childhood" *(Fan Ton)*. Principally, when the muscles in the area are exercised, the nerves and *Chi* channels will start to accumulate the energy which has been generated by the exercise. This kind of energy generation and accumulation is called "Starting the Fire" or *"Chi For"*. It is enhanced by concentrating the mind strongly on this activity. Later, it was found that in the *Chi For* exercise, the breathing must be coordinated in order to exercise the muscles efficiently and regularly. Also, this regular breathing coordination helps the meditator to concentrate his mind on the exercise. As explained in Chapter 1, the mind can control the *Chi's* generation and circulation. Therefore, in meditation, one should concentrate his mind at the *Dan Tien*, which is called *"Yi Sou Dan Tien"*, or "the mind always stays with the *Dan Tien*".

Because it is a principle of Chinese meditation that the *Dan Tien* is the source of *Chi* circulation, beginning training is centered around this spot. The first thing to learn to do is to control the abdominal muscles, making them expand and contract at will, so that the lower abdomen rises and falls like a baby's. This "Back to Childhood" exercise can be done by simply practicing frequently. Usually after one month of practicing 30 minutes daily, a person can accomplish this control. With continued practice, the exercise will generate more and more energy. By keeping the mind concentrated on the *Dan Tien*, the energy will concentrate there. When the accumulated *Chi* is strong enough, the meditator should be able to feel warmth in the *Dan Tien* area.

This back to childhood abdominal exercise will confer several benefits. First, the up and down motion of the abdominal muscles during deep breathing will massage the stomach and intestines as well as exercise the muscles holding the internal organs in place, and will increase their strength. This is the reason why deep breathing exercise can cure hernias, which are caused by weakness of the internal muscles. Second, exercising the abdominal muscles will generate *Chi* not only for circulation, but also directly for the organs held and surrounded by these muscles. This *Chi* supply plus the increased blood circulation keeps the organs healthy. Finally, the deep breathing uses the lungs to their fullest capacity, thereby strengthening and cleaning them.

If the meditator continues for another two to three weeks after the *Dan Tien* feels warm, he will then feel the muscles trembling or tingling. It is the accumulation of *Chi* in the nerves and *Chi* channels which causes the muscles to be out of control. This phenomenon is called *"Don Chu"* or Movement Sensing, in meditation. (As a matter of fact, the term *"Don Chu"* is used in meditation for any kind of perceptible phenomenon caused by *Chi* flow, redistribution, or overaccumulation. The most common experiences are itching, tingling or twitching of isolated muscles, or uncontrollable shaking of the whole body). When the lower abdominal muscles begin to vibrate, it is time to guide the energy or *Chi* to start its circulation. Concentration at this moment is extremely important. The meditator should be very calm and should not get excited by the *Don Chu* feeling. This phenomenon, however, does not happen to every meditator. For some the first cycling cavities are already open and the *Chi* will move through them without *Don Chu* happening.

Before going further, a meditator should understand first what the *Chi* cycling route or path is. As mentioned, there are two main vessels which are located on the front and back of the body (Figs. 3-3 and 3-4). The front vessel is called the Conception Vessel *(Ren Mei)*, which contains the *Yin* circulation. This vessel starts from the lower lip and extends down the front center of the body to the Sea Bottom cavity *(Hai Di)* between the scrotum or vagina and the anus. This cavity is called *Huiyin* (*Yin* Intersection) in acupuncture. The vessel on the back is called the Governing Vessel or *Du Mei*, and contains the *Yang* circulation. It starts from the Sea Bottom and follows the spine, passes up the back and over the top of the head and ends at the roof of the mouth. These two vessels are not connected at the top. However, when the tongue touches the roof of the mouth cavity, the *Yin* and *Yang* vessels are connected and the circuit is complete. This tongue touch is called *"Da Chiao"* or building the bridge. The tongue acts like a switch in an electrical circuit. If this bridge is not built, the circuit is not complete and the *Chi* circulation will be incomplete. Therefore, when a person meditates either in *Wai Dan* or in *Nei Dan*, he should keep his tongue touching the roof of the mouth all the time. Of course, everyone frequently touches the roof of the mouth with his tongue during everyday activities. However, in meditation, a continuous circuit is important. The tongue should be relaxed and lightly touch the center of the roof of the mouth (Fig. 3-5). If the tongue is tight, it will result in stagnation of the *Chi* flow. Also, the tongue should not touch the teeth, which will not connect the bridge efficiently, and very often makes the meditator feel sleepy. On the other hand the tongue should not be stretched to touch the back of the roof of the mouth. This will make the tongue muscles tight and sore and will also stagnate the *Chi* flow. If a meditator creates the tongue bridge properly, he will feel saliva secreted during meditation. He should swallow it to keep his throat moist. The spot on the center of the roof of the mouth where the tongue touches is called the *"Tien Tzie"* (Heaven's Pond), or *"Lung Chuan"* (Dragon Spring).

When the student can circulate the *Chi* through the two major vessels, he has completed the "Small Circulation" *(Shao Chou Tien)*. Usually, if one meditates three times a day for half an hour with the right method, he can complete this circulation in 90 days. However, it is not uncommon for a person to take longer. The time needed to accomplish this depends on the degree to

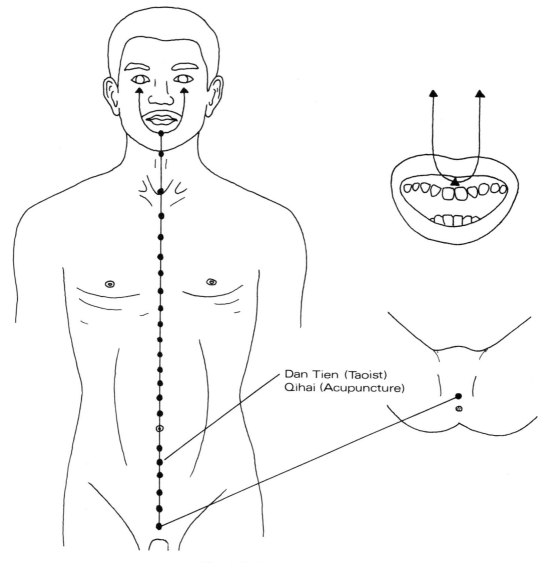

Fig. 3-3. Course of *Ren Mei*

which a person can concentrate, relax, understand the techniques and principles, and feel the *Chi* flow. It is very important that a meditator should not try to hurry the process, because this will make the circulation worse and might be dangerous.

The reader should understand that the *Chi* has been circulating all the time in his body. However, the *Chi* circulation can become stagnant or slow. The reason for this is that in the vessels and *Chi* channels there are many knots at which the channels are narrower or harder to penetrate. Usually, these knots are located at cavities. The main purpose of *Nei Dan* meditation is to open or widen these knots and enable the *Chi* to flow without stagnation. When *Chi* is stagnant and does not flow smoothly, a person will soon feel sick and the related organ will become weakened. When the *Chi* channels are open the arteries

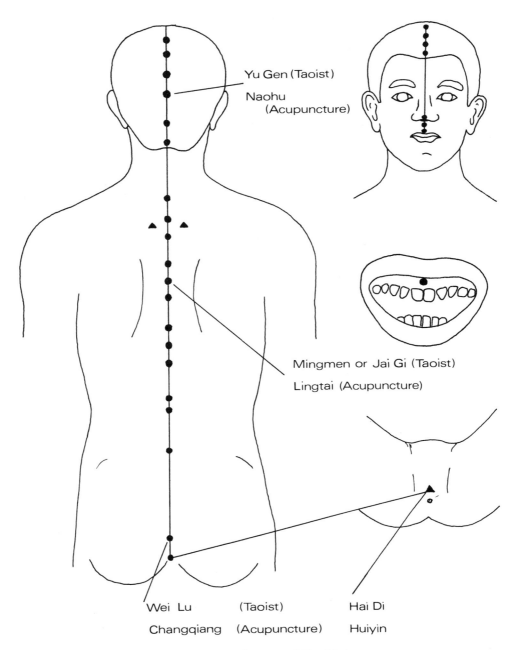

Yu Gen (Taoist)

Naohu
(Acupuncture)

Mingmen or Jai Gi (Taoist)

Lingtai (Acupuncture)

Wei Lu   (Taoist)   Hai Di

Changqiang   (Acupuncture)   Huiyin

Fig. 3-4. Course of *Du Mei*

will be open also and will allow the blood to flow smoothly. This is because the arteries usually follow the *Chi* channels. For this reason, the meditator will be able to cure high blood pressure.

In *Nei Dan* Small Circulation, there are three cavities or knots (see Fig. 3-4) which are harder to pass through than the others, and might cause difficulties. These are called the *"San Guan"* or Three Gates. The first cavity is called *"Wei Lu"* by the Taoists and *"Changqiang"* by the acupuncturists. It is located at

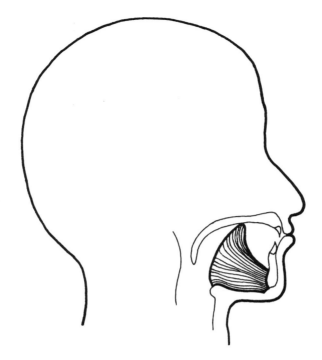

Fig. 3-5. Tongue Position

the tailbone. The second is called *"Jar Gi"* or *"Ming Men"* (Life's Door) by Taoists and *"Lingtai"* (Spiritual Tower) by acupuncturists. The last cavity is called *"Yu Gen"* (Jade Pillow) by Taoists and *"Naohu"* (Brain Door) by acupuncturists, and is located at the base of the skull. Further explanation of these three cavities will be given in the next section. These spots offer the greatest resistance to increased *Chi* flow and so are the three major milestones for judging progress in achieving the Small Circulation.

In controlling the *Chi's* movement in the circulation, the meditator should be able to feel that something is flowing, following the guidance of his mind. However, a meditator can also feel the back muscles beside the vessel expanding and tensing. This expanding feeling will not happen when the *Chi* goes above the Jade Pillow cavity at the back of the head. Instead, the meditator will feel only the energy or *Chi* flow, since there is no thick muscle on the head for the meditator to feel. The usual feeling of *Chi* flow on the head is local numbness or tickling, as though insects were brushing the skull.

During meditation, a meditator may naturally swing or move his body forward and backward. Sometimes he will feel a muscle jump or contract by itself. These are all symptoms of *Don Chu* caused by *Chi* redistribution. There is nothing to be alarmed about; this is all normal.

Once a meditator has accomplished the Small Circulation, he will then try to master the "Grand Circulation" which will circulate the energy to the entire body through the twelve *Chi* channels. Usually a meditator will either concentrate only on his arms or only on his legs first and then go to the other limbs. However, it is also common for the meditator, once he completes the Small Circulation, to practice guiding the *Chi* to the upper and lower limbs simultaneously and to imagine *Chi* expanding from the two main vessels.

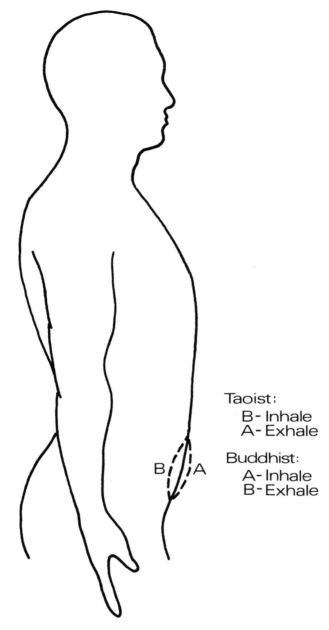

Taoist:
  B- Inhale
  A- Exhale

Buddhist:
  A- Inhale
  B- Exhale

B   A

Fig. 3-6. Abdominal Motion During Breathing

In the next section, both Buddhist and Taoist meditation methods will be discussed. Before a beginner starts his meditation, he should read this and the following sections repeatedly, until he is sure he understands them.

3-3. Nei Dan Practice
Small Circulation (Shao Chou Tien)
Meditation Breathing

The first and most important step for effective meditation is proper breathing. There are two basic methods in use in Chinese meditation: Taoist and Buddhist.

Taoist breathing, also known as reverse breathing *(Fan Fu Shih)*, is used to prepare the *Chi* for circulation, and its proper development is crucial. In Taoist breathing the normal movement of the lower abdomen is reversed during inhalation and exhalation. Instead of expanding when inhaling, the Taoist contracts, and vice versa (Fig. 3-6). One must never hold the breath or force the process. Inhale through the nose slowly, keeping the flow smooth and easy and contract and lift the lower abdomen up behind the navel. When the lungs are filled, begin to exhale gently. Inhalation is considered *Yin* and exhalation is considered *Yang*. They must operate together like the *Yin Yang* circle, one becoming the other smoothly and effortlessly in a fluid circular motion. As exhalation occurs, slowly push the *Dan Tien* and lower abdomen out. The area of the *Dan Tien* is where the *Chi* will be produced and accumulated in order to start the Small Circulation. Because of this, the muscles around the *Dan Tien* must be trained so that they can sufficiently contract and expand while the student inhales and exhales. At first expanding the lower abdomen while exhaling may be difficult; but with practice the muscles learn to expand more and more until the entire lower abdomen expands upon exhalation from the navel to the pubic bone. One should not force the *Dan Tien* to expand, but rather should work gently until success is achieved.

This whole process is a form of deep breathing, not because the breathing is heavy, but because it works the lungs to near capacity. While many people who engage in strenuous exercise breathe hard, they do not necessarily breathe deeply. Deep breathing causes the internal organs to vibrate in rhythm with the breath, which stimulates and exercises them. The organs would not receive this type of internal exercise without deep breathing. It can be seen that many forms of violent exercise only condition the external muscles, while doing very little for the vital organs.

In the Buddhist breathing method the movement of the abdomen is the opposite of the Taoist. When the meditator inhales, he expands it instead of withdrawing, and when he exhales, he contracts it (Fig. 3-7). This kind of breathing is called the normal breath *(Tsan Fu Shih)*. It is the same kind of breathing a singer practices.

Both methods use the same principle of *Chi* generation. The main difference is that the coordination of the abdominal motion with the breath is opposite. In fact many meditators can use either method, and switch very easily.

Meditation and Chi Circulation

Once the student can breathe adequately according to the Taoist and Buddhist methods, he begins sitting meditation to begin the process of *Chi* circulation. The first goal is to achieve a calm mind while concentrating on deep breathing. The individual creates a type of hypnotic state to do this. The meditator should stay at this stage until he can expand and withdraw his *Dan Tien* while breathing with no conscious effort, without the attention wandering.

When the muscles around the *Dan Tien* can be easily controlled, the process of breating acts as a pump to start a fire, which is *Chi* production, in the furnace of the *Dan Tien*. This whole process of generating and accumulating *Chi*

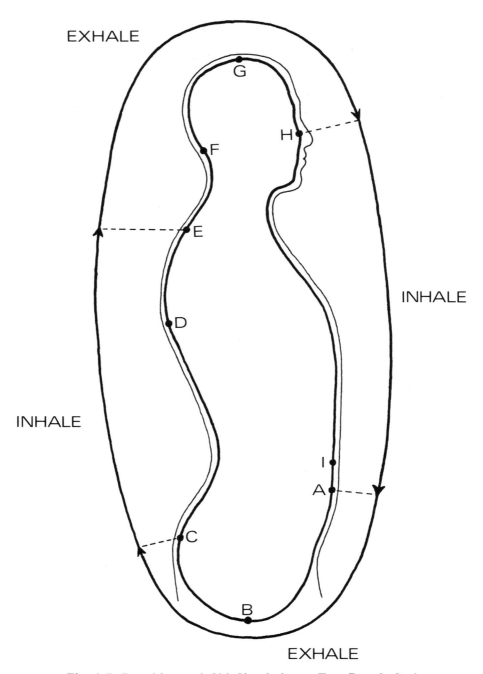

Fig. 3-7. Breathing and Chi Circulation -- Two Breath Cycle

in the *Dan Tien* is called lower level breathing *(Shar Chen Chi)*, while simple exhalation and inhalation in the lungs is called upper level breathing *(Sarn Chen Chi)*. One system aims at building *Chi* as energy, while the other aims at building up *Chi* as air. The overabundant *Chi* in the *Dan Tien* will cause the abdominal area in most people to twitch and feel warm. The pump (the deep breathing) has thus caused a fire (an accumulation of *Chi*) in the *Dan Tien* area. When this occurs, the *Chi* is ready to burst out of the *Dan Tien* and travel into another cavity.

In order to insure that the accumulated *Chi* passes into the correct cavity, the sitting posture must be correct (legs crossed). When the *Chi* is ready to burst from the *Dan Tien*, it must not be allowed to travel into the legs. By having the legs properly crossed, the *Chi* is partially blocked. If the *Chi* does go downward, it may stagnate in some of the cavities. For a novice meditator, this is dangerous, since he does not have enough experience or understanding of controlling *Chi* with his will. This *Chi* residue in the cavities will later affect the leg's *Chi* circulation, and might, in extreme cases, cause paralysis. When *Chi* goes into an undesired *Chi* channel and causes problems, it is called "*Dsou For*" or "Fire Deviation". Therefore, during any serious meditation session in which the practitioner attempts to circulate his *Chi*, the legs must be crossed. Only after the Small Circulation has been totally achieved and the meditator is attempting the Grand Circulation, is it permissible to uncross the legs.

In order to correctly initiate the Small Circulation the *Chi* must pass into the *Wei Lu* cavity, located in the tailbone. Thus, the *Chi* passes from the *Dan Tien* down through the groin area, called the Bottom of the Sea (*Hai Di*), and into the tailbone. The *Chi* does pass through other acupuncture cavities on the way to the *Wei Lu* (Fig. 3-4), but the *Wei Lu* will offer the greatest resistance because the bone structure narrows the channel.

During meditation the mind must guide the *Chi* consciously throughout its circulation. Without the mind consciously leading the circulation of *Chi*, there will be no consistent or smooth circulation. It sometimes happens that the *Chi* will pass from the *Dan Tien* into the *Wei Lu* without conscious effort, but the mind must actively guide the *Chi* for further results. Starting from the *Dan Tien*, the mind remains calm and fully concentrated only on guiding the *Chi* past the *Wei Lu*. This process must never be pushed. Simply keep the mind on the next cavity and let the *Chi* get there by itself. The requirement of concentration is one of the reasons why simple relaxation will only promote local circulation. For the larger circuits, the *Chi* must be guided by the will.

The secret of bringing the *Chi* to the *Wei Lu* point is to tighten the anus while inhaling. This is called "*Bi Gang*" (Close the Anus) in meditation. When exhaling, the anus is relaxed and *Chi* is guided to the *Wei Lu*. This is called "*Shon Gang*" (Relax the Anus). This coordination should be done even after the Small Circulation has been completed.

After the *Chi* has been successfully guided to the *Wei Lu*, it moves up the spine to the next major obstacle, the *Ming Men* (Gate of Life) or *Jar Gi* (Press Spine). This point is located on the back directly behind the heart between the spinous processes of the sixth and seventh thoracic vertebrae (Fig. 3-4). In acupuncture this same cavity is called *Lingtai* (Spiritual Tower). When *Chi* flows to this area, it will usually cause the heart to beat faster, which can interfere with concentration. To lose concentration here might result in the *Chi* dispersing here, which will normally cause a cold sweat, tensing of the nerves, and rapid breathing. If the *Chi* remains in the surrounding area, it will stagnate the *Chi* flow in that area, and disturb the heart function. However, if one relaxes, concentrates on the cavity, and remains calm, there is usually little resistance to the *Chi* flow here.

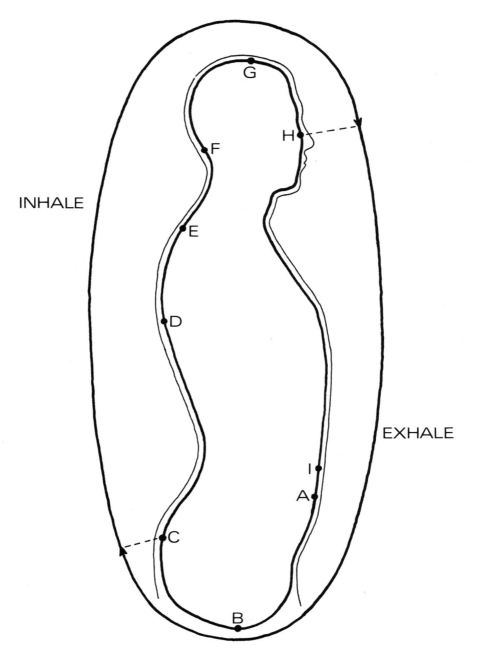

Fig. 3-8. Breathing and Chi Circulation -- One Breath Cycle

Once the *Chi* passes the *Ming Men*, the last major obstacle on the spine is called the *Yu Gen*, or Jade Pillow by meditators and *Naohu* by acupuncturists. This cavity is located at the base of the skull on top of the occipital bone (Fig. 3-4). Because of the skull structure, the channel is constricted here. If the energy does not pass smoothly through, it may pass into other channels on the head or into the brain. If this happens, one may experience headaches or feverish thinking.

Once the *Chi* enters the head, the sensation of *Chi* circulation is different from that of the circulation on the back. Circulation on the back causes the large spinal muscles to tense, and so it is pretty easy to feel. However, when the *Chi* enters the head, because the muscle layer there is very thin, no muscle tension will be felt. What will be felt is a tingling sensation, like insects walking, that will travel over the top of the head to the front of the face. The above three major cavities are called the Three Gates or *San Guan* in Chinese meditation.

After the *Chi* passes through the *Yu Gen*, the mind guides the *Chi* up over the top of the head, down the middle of the face and chest, and finally back to the *Dan Tien*, where the cycle starts over. When the complete cycle of the Small Circulation has been achieved, then the whole process is done continuously. Usually achieving the Small Circulation requires three sessions of meditation each day for a period of ninety or more days. The Grand Circulation may take years to achieve.

Up to this point little has been said about breathing during *Chi* circulation. Now that the background has been described, it can be added that the cyclic movement of *Chi* must be exactly coordinated with the deep breathing process. (Fig. 3-7) shows the basic pattern of Taoist meditation, which consists of guiding the *Chi* through one cycle of the Small Circulation during two sets of breaths (Table 3-1 lists the names of the important points and their corresponding abbreviations on Figs. 3-7, 3-8 and 3-9). This is the cycle that should be attempted by the beginner. To start, during the first inhalation the mind guides the *Chi* from the nose to the *Dan Tien*. Next, the practitioner exhales and guides the *Chi* from the *Dan Tien* to the *Wei Lu*. Then, he inhales and leads the *Chi* up to the point at the top of the shoulders, called the *Shun Bei* or *Dazhui*(see Table 3-1). Finally, the practitioner exhales and guides the *Chi* over the head to the nose to complete one cycle. Keep circulating the *Chi*, one cycle every two breaths.

After the two-breath cycle has been achieved, the student should go on to circulate his *Chi* in a one-breath cycle. This cycle is the basis for using *Chi* as the energy source in the martial arts. (Fig. 3-8) shows the one-breath cycle. The practitioner guides the *Chi* to the tailbone while exhaling, and then to the nose while inhaling.

Some beginning meditators say they cannot feel the *Chi* flow, while others say they feel it is stopped at a particular point. The answer to both of these is to keep on doing the cycle. At first, it will be mostly imagination and not much *Chi*, but with perseverance the flow will become stronger, more complete, and more perceptible. Remember that the *Chi* is always flowing or you would not be alive. Since *Chi* follows the mind, keeping the attention moving will keep the *Chi* flowing through the channels and gradually open the constrictions.

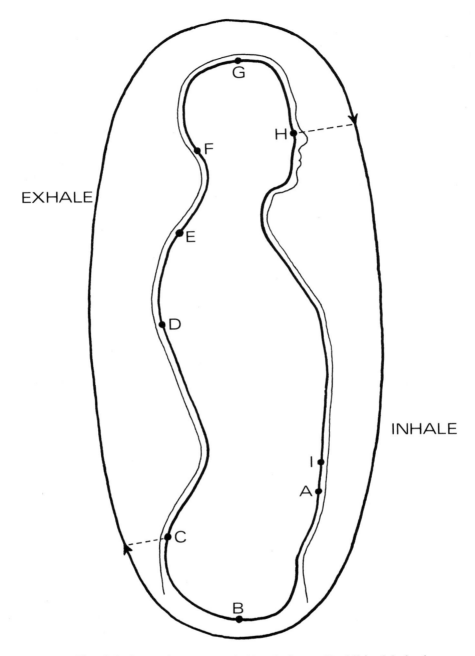

Fig. 3-9. Breathing and Chi Circulation -- Buddhist Method

Table 3-1

Point	Taoist Name	Acupuncture Name	Location
A	Dan Tien	Qihai	One and half inches below the navel
B	Hai Di	Huiyin	Pelvic floor
C	Wei Lu	Changqiang	Tailbone
D	Ming Men	Ling Tai	On the spine behind the heart
E	Shun Bei	Dazhui	Upper back
F	Yu Gen	Naohu	Base of the skull
G	Tien Lien Gai	Baihui	Crown of the skull
H	Bi	Suliao	Nose
I	Du Gi	Shenque	Navel

The advanced student can try reversing the current of *Chi* in the Small Circulation so that the *Chi* travels up the chest, over the top of the head, down the back, and then to the *Dan Tien*. In reverse circulation the stopping points of *Chi* between inhalation and exhalation remain the same. Thus, inhale and guide the *Chi* from the *Dan Tien* to the nose; next, exhale and guide the *Chi* over the head to the *Shun Bei*. The next step is to inhale and guide the *Chi* to the tailbone *(Wei Lu)* Finally, exhale and guide the *Chi* to the *Dan Tien*. The one-breath cycle follows the same principle. This reversed circulation can help heal injuries and can clear blockages that the regular circulation has difficulty passing through.

Included with the one-breath cycle described above is the Buddhist system of *Chi* circulation (Fig. 3-9). The Buddhist meditator inhales and guides his *Chi* from the nose, down the chest through the groin to the tailbone. Then he exhales and guides the *Chi* up the spine, then over the head to the nose. Buddhists can also reverse the direction of the cycle. The student should remember that in the Buddhist method the *Dan Tien* expands during inhalation and contracts during exhalation.

There are also methods of meditation that do not use the *Dan Tien* as the *Chi* source. Some systems use the solar plexus, the forehead, or other points, and generate *Chi* through concentration alone, without coordination with the breath.

Novice Meditators

The person who comes to meditation seriously for the first time should not attempt to circulate his *Chi* from the very start. The primary goal of the beginner must be to train the muscles around the *Dan Tien* so that the Taoist method of breathing is easy and natural. The training of the muscles is achieved through the preliminary practice of reverse breathing. Once the muscles have been adequately trained and the mind is sufficiently calmed, the novice may then attempt to circulate the *Chi*.

Pre-meditation Warm-up

Before meditation, the practitioner should spend three to five minutes calming his mind. Once the mind is calm he can begin concentrated meditation with better results. Calming the mind before meditation may be thought of as a warm-up exercise. For the more experienced meditator, the warm-up takes less time.

Fig. 3-10. Meditation Posture 1   Fig. 3-11. Meditation Posture 2

Posture

Two of the common cross-legged postures that are appropriate for meditation are shown in Figs. 3-10 and 3-11. The student should pick the one that
is most comfortable. In any posture the back should be straight without being
bolt upright; do not slouch. It is easiest to sit on a cushion about two inches
thick with the knees or feet on the floor at a lower level. This helps to keep
the back straight without strain.

If the legs become numb while sitting, uncross them and relax. With continued practice you will be able to sit comfortably longer and longer with the
legs feeling no discomfort. This usually takes several weeks. Sitting cross legged restricts the normal flow of blood and *Chi*, and the body needs to learn
to adjust to the new position.

In both sitting positions the hands should be held at the *Dan Tien*, one on
top of the other with the tips of the thumbs touching. This position helps you
to feel your breathing as you expand the *Dan Tien*, and to coordinate deep
breathing and *Chi* circulation. After you achieve the Small Circulation, you
may rest the backs of the hands on the knees with the thumbs and middle fingers
touching.

Geographical Positioning

You should face the east while meditating. This common practice was probably established because experienced meditators discovered empirically that their
Chi circulation was more fluid when they faced the east. This may happen
because the rotation of the earth enhances the flow of *Chi* slightly.

Time of Meditation

Ideally a person should meditate three times a day for one half hour at a
time. The best times to practice are 15 minutes before sunrise, one to two hours
after lunch, and one half hour before going to sleep. With this schedule the
meditator can, if he remains calm and concentrated, achieve the Small Circulation in about three months.

These three times have been found best because the morning and evening meditations take advantage of the changing of the body's energy from *Yin* to *Yang* or vice versa, and in the afternoon the individual is usually very relaxed.

If you can only meditate twice a day, skip the afternoon session. If only once, then meditate in either morning or evening. Reducing the number of sessions means taking longer to achieve the Small Circulation.

Thoughts

During meditation the mind should focus on the *Dan Tien* and on the circulation of *Chi*. The whole purpose of meditation is lost if the mind wanders. The student must achieve a relaxed hypnotic trance; this is easily done by concentrating on the rhythmic pattern of breathing. When the attention does stray, or when thoughts start arising, simply return your attention to the breathing.

If the individual has too many day-to-day worries bothering him during meditation, he should neither meditate nor attempt to circulate his *Chi*. Instead he should breathe deeply for relaxation. Attempting to *Chi* circulate while emotionally agitated can only harm the meditator.

Position of the Tongue, Teeth, and Eyes

During meditation, the tongue should lightly touch the roof of the mouth near the center. This creates a bridge between *Yin* and *Yang* and allows the *Chi* to circulate in a continuous path around the body. The student should take care that his tongue is neither too far forward nor too far back--both will hinder meditation. Too far forward causes sleepiness, too far backward hinders relaxation and the tension obstructs the *Chi* flow. The tongue bridge also allows saliva to accumulate in the mouth. This should be swallowed occasionally to lubricate the throat to keep it from getting too dry. In addition, the teeth should touch lightly.

The eyes can be either closed or kept half open during meditation, but the meditator should not let himself become sleepy if the eyes are closed.

The Mechanics of Meditation

Cautions:

There are a few general rules which will prevent the student from causing himself injury, and which will help to speed the process of meditation.

1. Don't smoke. Because meditation involves deep breathing, the lungs must be able to function adequately.
2. Don't drink too much. Too much alcohol will hurt the nervous system and hinder *Chi* circulation.
3. Wash before meditation. This will help relax the mind.
4. Wear loose, comfortable clothing, especially around the waist.
5. Meditate in a well ventilated place.
6. Avoid sex 24 hours before and after meditation (For men only).
7. Women should not concentrate on the *Dan Tien* during their periods, but instead should place their attention on the solar plexus.
8. Meditate in a quiet place with as little disturbance as possible.
9. Wait at least half an hour, preferably one or two hours after eating to meditate.
10. Do not meditate if you are worried or ill.
11. Never hold the breath.
12. Always remain relaxed while meditating.

13. Always concentrate on the *Dan Tien* and on the *Chi* flow.
14. If you repeatedly feel bad or get strongly unpleasant reactions during meditation, stop. Do not proceed without the guidance of a meditation master.

Common Problems
Numb legs:

This problem affects nearly everyone who begins sitting meditation, especially people who are unused to sitting cross legged. It is caused by a reduced flow of blood and *Chi* to the legs. The problem gradually goes away by itself. Until then the student should stop meditation when the numbness disturbs his concentration. Stretch out the legs to open the channels and use acupressure or massage on the arches of the feet to speed recovery. As soon as feeling returns, resume meditation.

Cavity pain:

Some meditators experience pain in the tailbone, at the kidneys, at the Life Door *(Ming Men),* or at the top of the thighs when *Chi* circulation reaches these spots. It is caused by increased pressure at that point, often because of a previous injury to that part of the body. The sensation is normal and can be relieved by relaxing more. Ordinarily this kind of pain will only last two or three days or until the circulation has passed that spot.

Headache:

This is caused by tension, worry, fatigue or when circulation first reaches the head. If it is caused by tension or worry, stop meditating until you calm down. If you are too tired to concentrate, it would be better to take a nap. If it is the result of *Chi* flow into the head, increase the concentration and relax more. The pain can be relieved by using the massages described in the next section.

Backache:

Backaches can be caused by either improper posture or by a residue of stagnant *Chi.* If the posture is too stiffly erect or if the meditator slumps, there will be too much tension in the back muscles and backache will result. To assume a comfortable posture, sit up very straight, stretching upward as far as possible, then relax without bending forward.

A residue of stagnant *Chi* is sometimes dangerous and should be treated with heavy massage. See the next section for a description of effective massage techniques.

Drowsiness:

Drowsiness is a result either of being too tired, in which case you should stop meditating, or of having the tongue too far forward in the mouth, in which case it should be placed further back.

Sweating:

If sweating is a result of the environment, if the place where you meditate is too hot or too humid, try to change it. If the sweating is not a result of environmental factors, there are two kinds, hot and cold. Cold sweats may indicate an injury to one of the cavities in the path of circulation. Consult a meditation master who can help to clear the obstruction. Hot sweats are usually caused by circulating the *Chi* without concentrating, and go away with improved concentration and relaxation.

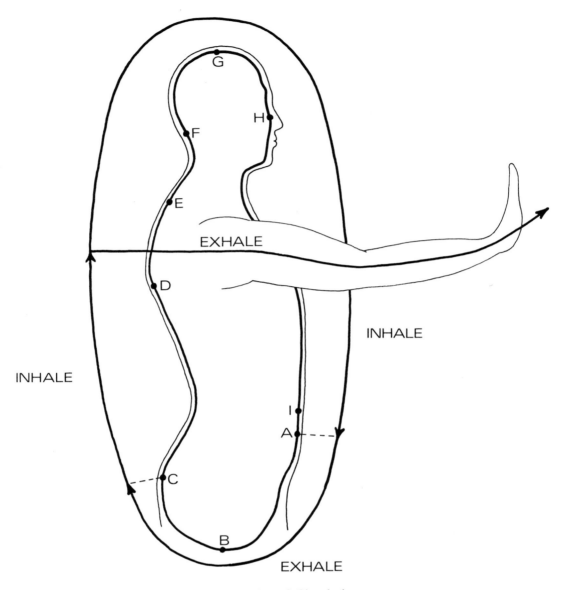

Fig. 3-12. Grand Circulation

Grand Circulation (Da Chou Tien)

The next step in training after the meditator can cycle his *Chi* in the two vessels at will is the Grand Circulation in which he cycles the *Chi* generated at the *Dan Tien* to the whole body through all the channels.

By this time the meditator should be able to feel the *Chi* generating and flowing around his body in the Small Circulation. With this as a basis he should be able to experience and accomplish the Grand Circulation easily and safely through mental control of the *Chi*.

In Grand Circulation training the whole body should be relaxed. If the meditator tries to circulate to his arms and hands, he can either sit in a chair or stand. As the meditator inhales, he brings the *Chi* from the tailbone up the back to the top of the shoulders (Fig. 3-12). Inhaling also prepares the *Chi* on

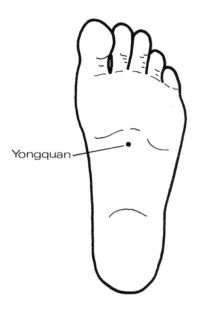

Fig. 3-13. *Yongquan* Cavity

the front of the body for a new cycle. As he exhales, he guides the *Chi* not over the head, but into the arms. At the same time that the *Chi* flows into the arms, the *Dan Tien* expands, starting a new cycle by moving the new *Chi* into the tailbone. When the meditator inhales again, he guides the *Chi* to the base of the neck while preparing for a new cycle on the front of the body. Thus the *Chi* cycle is a one way path in that it does not travel in a complete circle, but in a line that ends in the hands. This cycle is repeated continuously until the meditator can feel the flow to the center of the palms. In this exercise the thumb and little finger should be slightly tightened by pulling them back in order to restrict the *Chi* flow and force it to the palm. There are many methods of practicing circulation to the upper limbs. The reader should refer to the next section for descriptions. When the *Chi* approaches the palm, the meditator should be able to sense it and feel the warmth. After this is achieved the practitioner should then try to guide the *Chi* to the fingertips.

In actual fact the *Chi* does circulate back to the *Dan Tien*, but concentrating on only a one way flow will push the circulation out to the hands sooner and more strongly.

To circulate the *Chi* to the lower limbs, a common method is to lie down on your back and relax the leg muscles to open the *Chi* channels. Inhale and contract the abdomen, then exhale and guide the *Chi* through the legs to the Bubbling Well point *(Yongquan)*on the bottom of the feet (see Fig. 3-13). Normally the *Chi* channels in the legs are open wider than those in the arms. Consequently, it is easier to circulate to the legs than to the arms. When the *Chi* approaches the bottom of the feet, they will feel warm and numb, and this feeling may persist for several days the first time it is experienced.

Some teachers recommend following certain paths to and from the feet and hands. This is not really necessary. If you push the *Chi* into your feet and hands, it will find its own way there, and in time will fill your limbs, moving through all the channels, both *Ching* and *Lou*. Keep in mind, too, that the "pushing" is always gentle and relaxed.

Because the leg channels are wide, it is sometimes possible to circulate standing up, even though the muscles are slightly tight. This is the reason that *Tai Chi* practitioners can accomplish the Grand Circulation through the slow motion exercise.

After the meditator can circulate *Chi* to the arms and legs, he has achieved the Grand Circulation. This can take six months to achieve, or many years, depending on the person and the time he has available for practice.

Beyond the Grand Circulation, the meditator can develop the ability to expand the *Chi* to the arms and legs simultaneously, to expand the *Chi* in the form of a ball larger than the body, to take in *Chi* from outside the body, or direct the *Chi* at will to specific parts of the body, such as the palm, fingertips, or the area of an injury.

If someone learns to transport his *Chi* beyond his body or take in *Chi* from outside, then he might be able to use his *Chi Kung* to cure illness and injuries involving *Chi* disturbance. However, this should not be attempted without an experienced instructor's training. To take outside disturbed *Chi*, called evil *Chi* (*Shia Chi*) into your body without knowing how to get rid of it is dangerous. By the same token to extend your own *Chi* into another's body without knowing the proper stopping point, risks *Chi* exhaustion.

3-4. Chi Enhancement and Transport

Once a *Chi Kung* practitioner has accomplished his Grand Circulation, he will begin to practice advanced methods to make his *Chi* stronger, more focused, and more controlled by his will. Even though a practitioner can start this *Chi* enhancement after accomplishing the Small Circulation, the enhancement will be easier and more efficient if he waits until the completion of the Grand Circulation.

The first training method is called "*Lien Chi*"(Train the *Chi*) or "*Chun Chi*"(Filling *Chi*). The main purpose of this training is to make the *Chi* fill up the *Dan Tien* area, so that when *Chi* is accumulated there the abdomen is resilient like a balloon and can endure or resist a strong attack. As the *Chi* gets stronger and stronger in the *Dan Tien*, the *Chi* flow in the body also gets stronger and stronger. The training method of *Chun Chi* is simply to blow out a candle, starting two feet away and increasing the distance as you are able. Keep the tongue against the middle of the roof of the mouth while concentrating on the *Dan Tien*. Tighten the lips to form a very small opening. Blow the air out through this opening slowly and steadily, imagining that the stream of air is directed at the flame without spreading out at all. Blow as long as possible without straining. While blowing imagine that *Chi* is expanding and accumulating in the *Dan Tien*. When one can blow the candle out easily, he should then move the candle further away and continue. Practice five to ten minutes daily.

Another method of *Lien Chi*, called "*Kuar Chi*" (Expanding *Chi*), is to extend the *Chi* in a ball outward from the surface of the body. To do this the student should imagine while exhaling that his Chi is expanding out from the body in all directions forming a globe and that the center of the globe is the *Dan Tien*. When a meditator becomes proficient at this exercise, he will feel his body has disappeared, that he is transparent, and that he is a ball of *Chi* which gets smaller and smaller when inhaling and expands when exhaling. This exercise not only enhances the symmetrical movement of *Chi*, but also enables the *Chi* to reach every cell of the body simultaneously.

Fig. 3-14.

Fig. 3-15.

Fig. 3-16.

Fig. 3-17.

Fig. 3-18.

Fig. 3-19.

After *Chi* development is at a fairly strong level, the student can begin to learn to focus or concentrate his *Chi* at some small area of the body. This kind of training is called *"Yun Chi"* or transporting the *Chi*. The main use of *Yun Chi* training is in the martial arts, where the *Chi* is concentrated in the palms for attack. Also, *Chi* can be transported to a specific area to resist a blow or punch. This latter *Yun Chi* practice is part of "Iron Shirt" or "Golden Bell Cover" training (see Chapter 5).

Here a few training methods will be introduced. The first task is to learn to focus the *Chi* in the palm. In the beginning this will proceed slowly, but with practice it will happen instantaneously.

1. The first form is called *"Gung Sou"* or Arcing the Arms (Fig. 3-14), in which the arms form a circle in front of the body with the fingertips close together, but not touching. *Gung Sou* can be done either sitting or standing. When the practitioner exhales, he guides the *Chi* to the arms and fingertips and imagines

the energy exchánging at the fingers from one arm to the other. The *Chi* should flow to the hands from both arms at the same time, circling in both directions simultaneously.

2.   The second form is to hold the hands as if holding a basketball in front of the chest. The elbows should not bend too much, which will stagnate the flow at the elbow area (Figs. 3-15 through 3-17). The mind should guide the *Chi* through the air from both palms, exchanging energy as in (1) above. The palms should move about continuously as though rotating an imaginary ball to gain the feeling of the smooth *Chi* flow. Often *Tai Chi Chuan* practitioners practice this exercise while holding an actual ball to develop the feeling of a smooth, circular flow. As a matter of fact, the imaginary ball works as well, so that a real ball is not necessary.

3.   The third form is to touch the palms together lightly in front of the chest (Fig. 3-18), and to exchange the *Chi* from one palm to the other while exhaling.

4.   The finger touch is more advanced than the palm touch. Touch the fingertips together lightly in front of the chest (Fig. 3-19), and exhange energy between hands while exhaling.

Fig. 3-20.   Fig. 3-21.   Fig. 3-22.

5.   Horizontal circling *Chi* flow is called Wave Hands Like Clouds in *Tai Chi*. Hold the right forearm at chest level parallel to the ground with the palm facing inward in front of the breast bone, elbow slightly lower than the rest of the arm. Hold the left hand palm down at waist level in front of the body (Fig. 3-20). Exhale and turn the trunk smoothly to the right as far as possible while directing the *Chi* to the palms (Fig. 3-21). Exhange the hands while inhaling (Fig. 3-22) and turn to the other side while exhaling (Fig. 3-23). This sequence should be repeated continuously so that a flowing rhythm is established.

6.   Sinking palm training. There are two ways to do sinking palm training, one with the palms facing down (Fig. 3-24), the other with the edge of the hands facing down (Fig. 3-25). When exhaling, let the palms feel like they are sinking. Imagine pressing down a resistant object while using a little muscle tension. The will leads the *Chi* to the palm or to the edge of the hand. When inhaling, relax the tension.

Fig. 3-23.

Fig. 3-24.

Fig. 3-25.

Fig. 3-26.

Fig. 3-27.

7. Palm pushing training. There are three directions of pushing palm training.
    (a). Forward and inward (Figs. 3-26 and 3-27);
    (b). Out to the sides and from the sides in (Figs. 3-28 and 3-29);
    (c). Up and down with hands exchanging (Figs. 3-30 and 3-31); and
    (d). Up and down with both hands at once (Figs. 3-32 and 3-33).
To practice, with each exhalation imagine pushing with the palms against a resistant object and guiding the *Chi* to the palm with slight muscle tension. Push a real wall to experience the feeling of real resistance at first.

    Other than the above seven forms of *Chi* transport and concentration training, there are two other common ways of practicing, both of which involve using a candle. The first way is the secret sword *Chi* transport (Fig. 3-34). To do this, hold both hands in the secret sword form, and point one of them at a candle flame. Begin with the fingertips one to two inches away. While exhaling, transport the *Chi* to the flame to make the flame move. If you practice

Fig. 3-28.

Fig. 3-29.

Fig. 3-30.

Fig. 3-31.

Fig. 3-32.

Fig. 3-33.

Fig. 3-34.

Fig. 3-35.

Fig. 3-36.

Fig. 3-37.

Fig. 3-38.

faithfully for quite a while you will be rewarded by being able to make the flame bend away from you. The second way of training is again to make the candle flame bend, but this time with the palm held five to ten inches away (Fig. 3-35). This is similar to the secret sword form, except that this time the *Chi* is directed out from the palm instead of the finger. Either way the hand not being pointed toward the flame should be kept in the same form and held in front of the waist for symmetry. Make sure when you do these exercises that your breath is directed away from the candle, and that only the *Chi* flow moves the flame.

3-5. Massage and Exercises after Meditation

After meditation or *Chi* transport training, the student should massage himself and do some loosening up exercises. The main purpose of massage is to loosen and relax the muscles on the *Chi's* paths. This can help the practitioner to clear the mind, and can also help to eliminate any residue of *Chi* which might remain in certain cavities. This residue of stagnant *Chi*, if left in the cavities, can affect normal *Chi* circulation and cause muscle and cavity pain. If a partner is available, it is best to massage each other, because it is easier to relax that way. Furthermore, a partner can massage the path on the back, which is difficult to do by yourself.

Fig. 3-39.

Fig. 3-40.

Fig. 3-41.

Fig. 3-42.

Massage

Head:

Begin with the face. Rub the ridge of the brow starting at the nose (Fig. 3-36) and moving the hands up and across the forehead until the fingers pass the temple (Fig. 3-37). Next put the hands under the eyes (Fig. 3-38) and rub across the cheeks. Third, put the thumbs in front of the ears (Fig. 3-39) and move the thumbs down to the chin. For the top of the head, place the fingers one inch off the centerline of the skull (Fig. 3-40). Move the scalp back and forth lightly over the skull. Reset the fingers along the same lines, but toward the back, and gently rub again. Keep moving the fingers back along the head and massaging until the back of the skull is reached. The last place to rub in the head area is the neck. Place the thumbs at the base of the skull and rub downward with the hands (Fig. 3-41).

Hands:

Rub the palms together (Fig. 3-42) then rub the center of the palm with the thumb (Fig. 3-43). In the center of the palm is a cavity which lies on the pericardium channel. By massaging this cavity, the heart is gently stimulated.

Kidneys:

Form fists with both hands and place the tops of the fists on the back behind the kidneys. Rub in a circular motion (Fig. 3-44).

Knees:

During meditation the knees may become stiff and absorb cold air through the pores. To warm them up and relieve the stiffness, use the open hand to rub around the whole joint (Fig. 3-45).

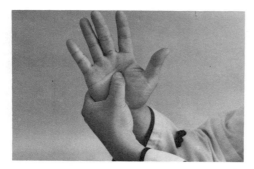

Fig. 3-43.

Fig. 3-44.

Fig. 3-45.

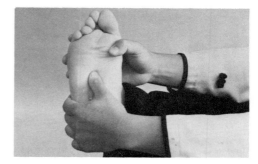

Fig. 3-46.

Feet:
　Rub the center of the bottom of the foot with the thumb (Fig. 3-46). This stimulates the kidneys via the kidney channel. You may then massage the whole bottom of the foot.

Exercises
1.　Rotate the head by slowly turning it from side to side without moving the rest of the body (Fig. 3-47).
2.　Rotate the back by slowly twisting the trunk from side to side while maintaining the sitting position (Fig. 3-48).
3.　Stretch the chest by clasping the hands behind the back and thrusting the chest as far forward as possible (Fig. 3-49).
4.　Rotate the shoulders forward and backward (Figs. 3-50 and 3-51).
5.　Lock the fingers with the palms facing out, then stretch the arms out in front (Fig. 3-52) and over the head (Fig. 3-53).
6.　Stretch the legs by grasping the feet and straightening the legs (Fig. 3-54).

Fig. 3-47.

Fig. 3-48.

Fig. 3-49.

Fig. 3-50.

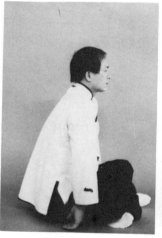
Fig. 3-51.

Fig. 3-52.

Fig. 3-53.

Fig. 3-54.

Fig. 3-55.

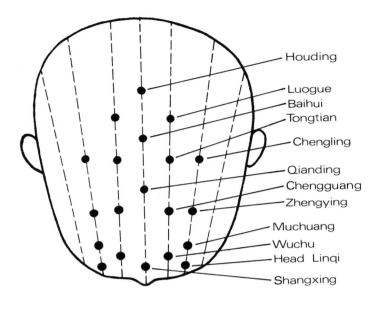

Houding
Luogue
Baihui
Tongtian
Chengling
Qianding
Chengguang
Zhengying
Muchuang
Wuchu
Head Linqi
Shangxing

Fig. 3-56. Acupuncture Cavities on the Crown of the Head

Beating the Drum (Min Gu)

The *Min Gu* exercise is very important in *Chi Kung* training. In this exercise the fingertips tap the top and back of the head, or the crown and Jade Pillow (*"Yu Gen"*) (Fig. 3-55), especially on the acupuncture points (Fig. 3-56). When the crown is tapped this way the resulting stimulation to the *Chi* channels and nervous system helps to increase circulation of *Chi* and blood in the head area. *Min Gu* should always be practiced after meditation for two reasons. First it helps one to awaken completely from the meditative state, and second it helps to flush away any *Chi* accumulated in the head during meditation. *Min Gu* can also be used in everyday life. After a long period of concentration it helps to clear the mind the same as after meditation. The Taoists have found that tapping the head not only clears and calms the mind, but also improves the memory and judgment. This is because the stimulation increases the supply of nutrients to the brain. *Min Gu* is helpful for relieving headache, especially tension headaches, again because of the increase in the flow of *Chi*. Finally, *Min Gu* can improve the health of the scalp if practiced regularly, and prevent loss of hair and graying.

Knocking the Teeth (Kou Tshi)

Kou Tshi is commonly used together with *Min Gu* after meditation. It consists of simply biting vigorously (but not too hard) about 50 times. It assists in clearing the mind and also promotes the health of the teeth by stimulating their roots. In addition, the knocking causes reverberations in the skull which helps to clear the mind.

CHAPTER 4
CHI KUNG & HEALTH

4-1. Introduction

Chi Kung was originally researched and developed by the Chinese to promote good health. For more than 4000 years they have investigated human *Chi* circulation, its relationship with the seasons, weather, and time of day. They have found that *Chi* is closely related to the altitude, location, food, emotional state, and even the sounds a person makes. They have done much research into methods of keeping the *Chi* circulation naturally healthy. These methods can roughly be divided into the categories of maintenance and healing. The first category specifies methods which can be used to maintain a person's health, and minimize the degeneration of the organs in order to increase the lifespan. The second specifies techniques which can be used to cure illnesses.

For maintenance *Chi Kung* the *Chi* is built up either by *Wai Dan* or *Nei Dan*, and then guided by the mind to circulate through the entire body. According to acupuncture theory, smooth *Chi* circulation is the key to health. When *Chi* is stagnant in a channel, the related organ will be weakened and will degenerate.

For curative *Chi Kung* methods, techniques are applied by patients to control the *Chi* circulation and gradually heal the disordered internal organs, or cure an external injury. The most generally used methods for doing this are acupuncture, masssage, and rubbing. Although *Wai Dan* and *Nei Dan* are primarily used to maintain smooth, abundant *Chi* circulation, advanced meditators sometimes use them to eliminate internal bruises and *Chi* stagnation caused by injuries. Recently, it has been found in China that *Wai Dan* and *Nei Dan* can be used to cure some cancers.

From acupuncture theory we know that the *Chi* channels are distributed over the entire body. These channels are closely related to the internal organs and are also related and connected to each other. All these channels have terminals at the hands, feet or head. Because of this fact, the Chinese doctor looks at the patient's face, tongue, and eyes and feels the pulses in the wrist to understand the severity of the illness and its prognosis.

For the same reason, a person can also stimulate the *Chi* circulation by massaging the ears, hands, and feet to gradually recover or increase the health of the *Chi* circulation. These reflexology techniques have proven very effective.

In this chapter the diagnostic techniques of Chinese physicians will be briefly described in section two. The theory and techniques of acupuncture will be discussed in section three. The reader who wishes more depth of coverage should refer to specialized texts on these subjects. In section four the theory and techniques of massage will be introduced, and skin rubbing methods will be summarized as well.

4-2. Chinese Diagnosis

When a person is sick, his *Chi* circulation is irregular or abnormal—it has too much *Yin* or too much *Yang*. Because all *Chi* channels are connected to the surface of the body, stagnant or abnormal *Chi* flow will cause signs to show on the skin. Also, the sounds a sick person makes when speaking, coughing, or breathing are different from those of a healthy person. Chinese doctors therefore examine a patient's skin, particularly the forehead, eyes, ears, and tongue. They also pay close attention to the person's sounds. In addition, they ask the patient a number of questions about his daily habits, hobbies, and feelings to understand the background of the illness. Finally, the doctor feels the pulses and probes special spots on the body to further check the condition of specific channels. Therefore, Chinese diagnosis is divided into four principal categories: 1)Looking *(Wang Chen)*; 2)Listening and Smelling *(Wen Chen)*; 3)Asking *(Wenn Chen)*; and 4)Palpation *(Chei Chen)*.

Obviously Chinese medicine takes a somewhat different approach to diagnosis than Western medicine does. Chinese doctors treat the body as a whole, analyzing the cause of the illness from the patient's appearance and behavior. Often what the Chinese physician considers important clues or causes are viewed by the Western doctor as symptomatic or irrelevant, and vice versa.

Next, we will briefly discuss the above four Chinese diagnostic techniques.
1.   Looking: (Wang Chen)-Looking at the spirit and inspecting the color.

(a) General Appearance: Examine the facial expression, muscle tone, posture, and general spirit.

(b) Skin Color: Examine the skin color of the injured area, if the problem is externally visible, like a bruise or pulled muscle. Examine the skin color of the face (Fig. 4-1). Since some channels are connected to the face, its color can tell the Chinese doctor what organs are disordered or out of balance.

(c) Tongue: The tongue is closely connected through channels with the heart, kidney, stomach, liver, gall bladder, lungs, and spleen (Fig. 4-2). In making his diagnosis, the Chinese doctor will check the shape, fur, color, and the body of the tongue to determine the condition of the organs.

(d) Eyes: From the appearance of the eyes a doctor can tell the liver condition. For example, when the eyes are red, it means the liver has too much *Yang*. Also, black spots on the whites of the eyes (Fig. 4-3), can tell of problems with the *Chi* circulation, degeneration of organs, or stagnancy due to an old injury.

(e) Hair: The condition of the hair can indicate the health of the kidneys and the blood. For example, thin, dry hair indicates deficient kidney *Chi* or weak blood.

(f) Lips and Gums: The color of the lips and their relative dryness indicates if the *Chi* is deficient or exhausted. Red, swollen, or bleeding gums can be caused by stomach fire. Pale, swollen gums and loose teeth might be a symptom of deficient kidneys.
2.   Listening and Smelling:

(a) Listen to the patient's breathing, mode of speech and cough. For example, a dry, hacking cough is caused by dry heat in the lungs.

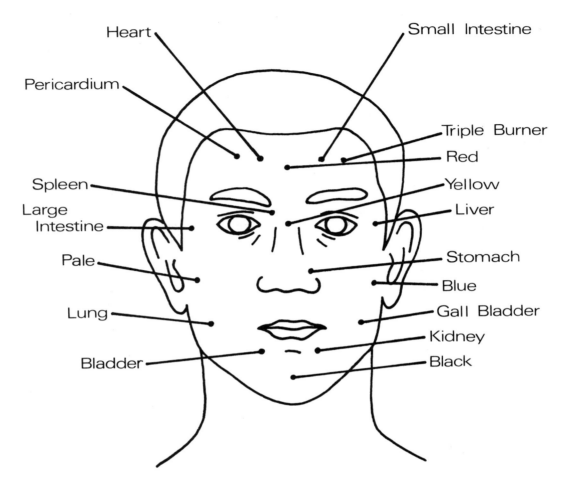

Fig. 4-1.

(b) Smelling the odor of a patients breath and excrement. For example, in the case of diseases caused by excessive heat, the various secretions and excretions of the body have a heavy, foul odor, while in diseases caused by excessive cold, they smell more like rotten fish.

3. Asking: This is one of the most important sources of a successful diagnosis. The questions usually cover the patient's past medical history, present condition, habits and life-style. Traditionally, there are ten main subjects a Chinese doctor will focus on in this interview. These are: a) Chills and fever, b) Head and body, c) Perspiration, d) Diet and appetite, e) Urine and stool, f) Chest and abdomen, g) Eyes and ears, h) Sleep, i) Medical history, and j) Bearing and living habits.

4. Palpation: There are three major forms of palpation (touching or feeling) in Chinese medicine:

(a) The palpation of areas which feel painful, hot, swollen, etc. to determine the nature of the problem. For example, swelling and heat indicates there is too much *Yang* in the area.

(b) The palpation of specific acupuncture points on the front and back of the trunk. For example, if the doctor senses a collapsed feeling, or the point is sore to the touch, this indicates the possibility of disease in the organ with which the point is associated.

(c) The palpation of pulse: Traditionally, the radial area pulse on the wrist (Fig. 4-4) is the principal site for pulse diagnosis. Although the pulse is specially related to the lungs and controlled by the heart, it reflects the condition of all organs (Table 4-1). The doctor checks the following: the depth (floating or submerged), the pace (slow or fast), the length (long or short), the strength (weak or strong), and the quality (slippery, rough, wiry, tight, huge, fine, or irregular). Usually it takes several years and hundreds of cases to become expert in the palpation of pulse.

Recently inspection of skin eruptions on the ears has been used in Chinese diagnosis. A number of sites have been found on the ear (Fig. 4-5) which become spontaneously tender or otherwise react to disease or injury somewhere in the body. Stimulation of these ear points in turn exerts certain therapeutic effects on those parts of the body with which they are associated.

This section serves only as a brief introduction to Chinese medical diagnosis. Interested readers should refer to books about Chinese medicine for more information.

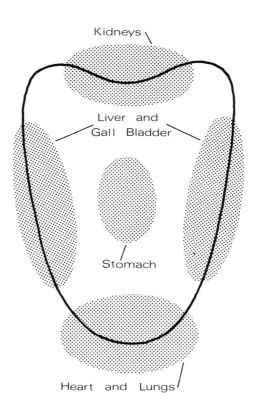

Fig. 4-2.

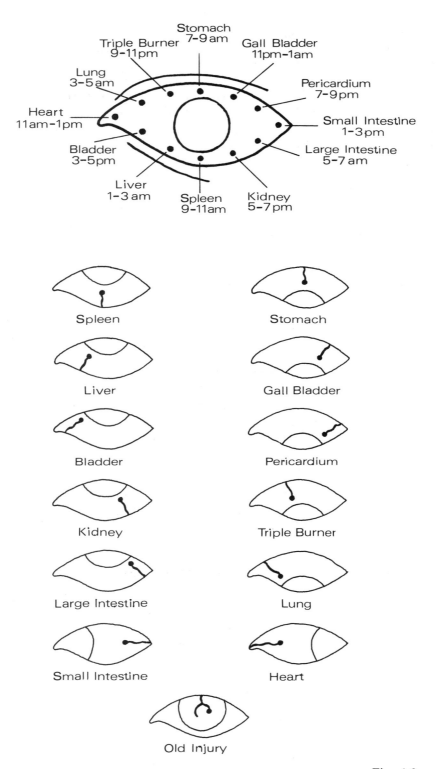

Fig. 4-3.

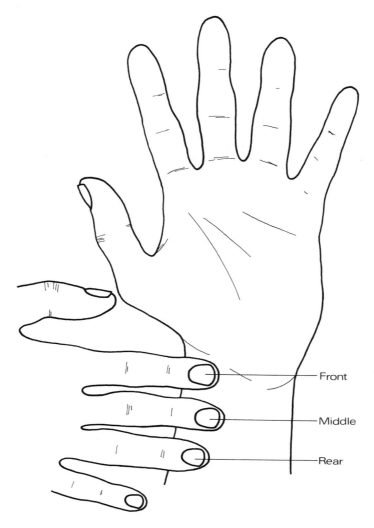

Fig. 4-4.

Table 4-1
The Palpation of Pulse

Left Hand	Organs
Rear	Kidney *Yin*
Middle	Liver
Front	Heart
Right Hand	**Organs**
Rear	Kidney *Yang*
Middle	Spleen
Front	Lungs

4-3. Acupuncture

In this section we will discuss how acupuncture is used, and why it works. Since *Chi Kung* exercises and *Chi* circulation theory are based on the results of acupuncture research, we believe this short theory summary will help the *Chi Kung* practitioner to understand the theory of the exercise.

The Relationship between the Points
of the Left Ear
and Surface Anatomical Structures

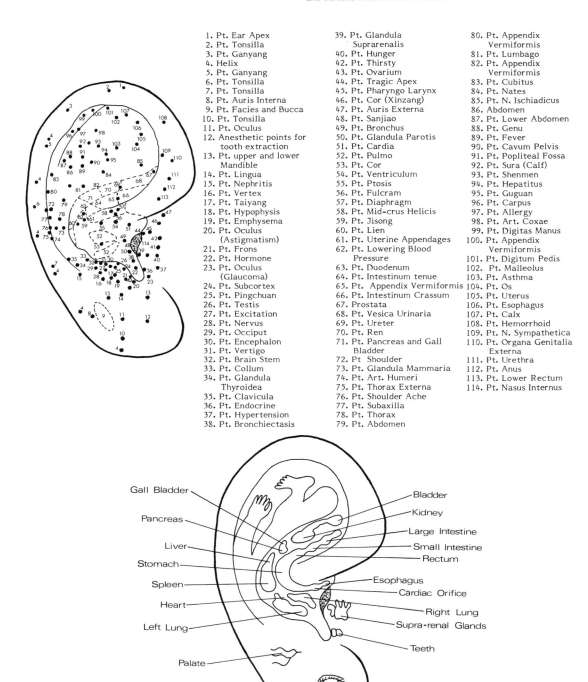

1. Pt. Ear Apex
2. Pt. Tonsilla
3. Pt. Ganyang
4. Helix
5. Pt. Ganyang
6. Pt. Tonsilla
7. Pt. Tonsilla
8. Pt. Auris Interna
9. Pt. Facies and Bucca
10. Pt. Tonsilla
11. Pt. Oculus
12. Anesthetic points for tooth extraction
13. Pt. upper and lower Mandible
14. Pt. Lingua
15. Pt. Nephritis
16. Pt. Vertex
17. Pt. Taiyang
18. Pt. Hypophysis
19. Pt. Emphysema
20. Pt. Oculus (Astigmatism)
21. Pt. Frons
22. Pt. Hormone
23. Pt. Oculus (Glaucoma)
24. Pt. Subcortex
25. Pt. Pingchuan
26. Pt. Testis
27. Pt. Excitation
28. Pt. Nervus
29. Pt. Occiput
30. Pt. Encephalon
31. Pt. Vertigo
32. Pt. Brain Stem
33. Pt. Collum
34. Pt. Glandula Thyroidea
35. Pt. Clavicula
36. Pt. Endocrine
37. Pt. Hypertension
38. Pt. Bronchiectasis

39. Pt. Glandula Suprarenalis
40. Pt. Hunger
42. Pt. Thirsty
43. Pt. Ovarium
44. Pt. Tragic Apex
45. Pt. Pharyngo Larynx
46. Pt. Cor (Xinzang)
47. Pt. Auris Externa
48. Pt. Sanjiao
49. Pt. Bronchus
50. Pt. Glandula Parotis
51. Pt. Cardia
52. Pt. Pulmo
53. Pt. Cor
54. Pt. Ventriculum
55. Pt. Ptosis
56. Pt. Fulcram
57. Pt. Diaphragm
58. Pt. Mid-crus Helicis
59. Pt. Jisong
60. Pt. Lien
61. Pt. Uterine Appendages
62. Pt. Lowering Blood Pressure
63. Pt. Duodenum
64. Pt. Intestinum tenue
65. Pt. Appendix Vermiformis
66. Pt. Intestinum Crassum
67. Pt. Prostata
68. Pt. Vesica Urinaria
69. Pt. Ureter
70. Pt. Ren
71. Pt. Pancreas and Gall Bladder
72. Pt Shoulder
73. Pt. Glandula Mammaria
74. Pt. Art. Humeri
75. Pt. Thorax Externa
76. Pt. Shoulder Ache
77. Pt. Subaxilla
78. Pt. Thorax
79. Pt. Abdomen

80. Pt. Appendix Vermiformis
81. Pt. Lumbago
82. Pt. Appendix Vermiformis
83. Pt. Cubitus
84. Pt. Nates
85. Pt. N. Ischiadicus
86. Abdomen
87. Pt. Lower Abdomen
88. Pt. Genu
89. Pt. Fever
90. Pt. Cavum Pelvis
91. Pt. Popliteal Fossa
92. Pt. Sura (Calf)
93. Pt. Shenmen
94. Pt. Hepatitus
95. Pt. Guguan
96. Pt. Carpus
97. Pt. Allergy
98. Pt. Art. Coxae
99. Pt. Digitas Manus
100. Pt. Appendix Vermiformis
101. Pt. Digitum Pedis
102. Pt. Malleolus
103. Pt. Asthma
104. Pt. Os
105. Pt. Uterus
106. Pt. Esophagus
107. Pt. Calx
108. Pt. Hemorrhoid
109. Pt. N. Sympathetica
110. Pt. Organa Genitalia Externa
111. Pt. Urethra
112. Pt. Anus
113. Pt. Lower Rectum
114. Pt. Nasus Internus

Gall Bladder
Pancreas
Liver
Stomach
Spleen
Heart
Left Lung
Palate
Eye

Bladder
Kidney
Large Intestine
Small Intestine
Rectum
Esophagus
Cardiac Orifice
Right Lung
Supra-renal Glands
Teeth

Fig. 4-5.

In order to understand acupuncture, one should know first what *"Ching"* and *"Lou"* are. Then he should understand what their function in the body is and their relationship to health. *"Ching"* and *"Lou"* are the *Chi* channels which connect the inside to the surface of the body, and which relate the internal organs to each other. They correspond with the vascular system with its arteries, veins, and capillaries. *"Ching"* are the main *Chi* channels which are distributed in the body, and are the paths of *Chi* and blood circulation. Usually, these *Ching* are found under a thick layer of muscle, and so are protected from the external influence, the same way the arteries and main nerves are are. There are twelve main *Ching* which connect the internal organs with the rest of the body. *"Lou"* are the minor *Chi* channels which connect the *Ching* to the surface of the body.

In addition to *Ching* and *Lou* , there are eight vessels which serve as balancing channels. These vessels also circulate *Chi*, however their function is different from *Ching* and *Lou* and they are called the "Strange *Ching* of the eight vessels" (*"Chi Ching Ba Mei"*). Among these eight vessels the *Ren* and *Du* vessels are most important.

Acupuncture theory classifies the internal organs into two kinds, viscera and bowels. According to Chinese theory, viscera are the organs which store essential substances for the body's use. These are the lungs, kidney, liver, heart, spleen, and pericardium. The bowels are organs which do not store substances, but eliminate them, being essentially hollow. These are the large intestine, gall bladder, urinary bladder, small intestine, stomach, and triple burner (*"Sanjiao"*). Viscera are *Yin*, while bowels are *Yang*, and they are grouped in pairs which are closely related with each other. It is important to note that in Chinese medicine, the term organ refers more to the functional system of that organ than to the actual physical lump of flesh. Hence, two of the organs in the Chinese system, the pericardium and the triple burner, have no corresponding organ in the Western system at all.

In classifying channels there are six degrees of *Yin* and *Yang* used to describe the six that terminate in the hands and the six that end in the feet.
The *Yin* channels are *Taiyin*, *Shaoyin*, and *Jueyin*. *Taiyin* is the very strongest most vigorous *Yin*. *Shaoyin* contains some *Yang*, and *Jueyin* is exhaused *Yin* and is found where two *Yin* channels meet. The *Yang* channels are *Taiyang*, *Shaoyang*, and *Yangming*. *Taiyang* is very strong, young *Yang*. *Shaoyang* is *Yang* that has begun to deteriorate, and *Yangming* is extreme *Yang*, and is found where two *Yang* channels meet.

In *Yin* and *Yang* theory, *Yang* is characterized by the outside of things, while *Yin* is the inside. In consonance with this principle, the twelve channels are considered *Yin* or *Yang* depending whether they are found on the inside or on the outside of the arm or leg. There are three *Yin* channels on the inside of each arm and leg, and three *Yang* channels on the outside. Of the two main vessels which make up the small circulation the *Ren*, which is found on the front of the body, is considered *Yin*, and the *Du*, which is found on the back, is considered *Yang*.

Chi circulates within this system continuously from the surface to the interior and back to the surface. The paths of the channels are as follows:

Upper Limb-*Yin Ching*: movement is from the chest to the hand

Hand *Taiyin*:   Runs from the top of the chest, along the inside of the arm, and ends on the outside of the thumb.

Hand *Shaoyin*:   Runs from the armpit, down the inside of the arm, and ends in the little finger.

Hand *Jueyin*:   Starts in the chest, runs up the chest, then down the middle of the inner arm and ends at the middle finger.

Upper Limb-*Yang Ching*: movement is from the hand to the head.

Hand *Taiyang*:   Starts at the end of the little finger, then runs up the outside of the arm, behind the shoulder, across the neck, and ends in front of the ear.

Hand *Shaoyang*:   Starts at the tip of the ring finger, then runs up the outside of the arm, around the shoulder, over the ear, and ends near the outside of the eyebrow.

Hand *Yangming*:   Starts at the tip of the index finger, runs along the outside of the arm, and ends near the nose.

Lower Limb-*Yin Ching*: movement is from the foot to the chest.

Foot *Taiyin*:   Starts at the tip of the big toe, runs up the inside of the leg, and ends at the top of the chest.

Foot *Shaoyin*:   Starts under the little toe, rises along the inside of the leg, and ends near the collarbone.

Foot *Jueyin*:   Starts on the outside of the big toe, then the inside of the leg, up the trunk, and ends near the nipple.

Lower Limb-*Yang Ching*: movement is from the head to the foot.

Foot *Taiyang*:   Starts at the inner corner of the eye, runs over the head, splits and runs in two channels down the back, joins on the back of the thigh and ends on the little toe.

Foot *Shaoyang*:   Starts at the outer corner of the eye, travels over the head, around the back of the shoulder, down the side of the chest and the outside of the leg, and ends in the fourth toe.

Foot *Yangming*:   Starts under the eye, runs down the front of the body, then down the outer front of the leg, and ends up in the second toe.

Ching are connected with one another at the extremities, where *Yin* meets *Yang*, and at the chest and face, where *Yin* meets *Yin* and *Yang* meets *Yang* (see Table 4-2). For the purposes of this table, the circuit starts above the nipples, moving through the channels in the order shown. Remember that there are two symmetrical systems, one on each side of the body.

Table 4-2
Order of Chi Circulation

From	To	Channel	Name	Time Period
Top of Chest	Outside of Thumb	Hand *Taiyin*	Lung	3 to 5 A.M.
Tip of Index Finger	Side of Nose	Hand *Yangming*	Large Intestine	5 to 7 A.M.
Under the Eye	Second Toe	Foot *Yangming*	Stomach	7 to 9 A.M.
Big Toe	Top of Chest	Foot *Taiyin*	Spleen	9 to 11 A.M.
Armpit	Little Finger	Hand *Shaoyin*	Heart	11 to 1 P.M.
Little Finger	Front of Ear	Hand *Taiyang*	Small Intestine	1 to 3 P.M.
Inner Corner of Eye	Little Toe	Foot *Taiyang*	Bladder	3 to 5 P.M.
Little Toe	Collarbone	Foot *Shaoyin*	Kidney	5 to 7 P.M.
Chest	Middle Finger	Hand *Jueyin*	Pericardium	7 to 9 P.M.
Ring Finger	Outside of Eyebrow	Hand *Shaoyang*	Triple Burner	9 to 11 P.M.
Outside Corner of the Eye	Fourth Toe	Foot *Shaoyang*	Gall Bladder	11 to 1 A.M.
Outside of Big Toe	Side of Nipple	Foot *Jueyin*	Liver	1 to 3 A.M.

Acupuncture theory also relates the organs to the five elements *(Wu Hsing)*: metal, wood, water, fire, and earth. These relationships are shown in Table 4-3 and Fig. 4-6. The five element theory is used to describe how organ systems influence each other through constructive and destructive sequences.

Table 4-3

Five Elements	Metal	Water	Wood	Fire	Earth	Mutual Fire
Yang Channels (External)	Hand *Yangming*	Foot *Taiyang*	Foot *Shaoyang*	Hand *Taiyang*	Foot *Yangming*	Hand *Shaoyang*
Bowels	Large Intestine	Bladder	Gall Bladder	Small Intestine	Stomach	Triple Burner
Yin Channels (Internal)	Hand *Taiyin*	Foot *Shaoyin*	Foot *Jueyin*	Hand *Shaoyin*	Foot *Taiyin*	Hand *Jueyin*
Viscera	Lung	Kidney	Liver	Heart	Spleen	Pericardium

From the *Chi* circulation and its relationship to the environment, the Chinese physicians found that a healthy person should not be too *Yin* or too *Yang*. When a person is ill, the acupuncturist will use needling or a few other methods to regulate the *Chi* flow and bring the person back to health. The reader should understand that it is not only the cavities lying on the channel corresponding to the afflicted organ that are used. Since the channels are interconnected and affect each other in various ways, cavities throughout the body are used to

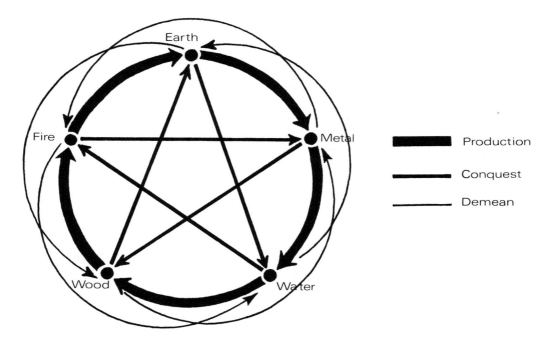

Fig. 4-6.

rebalance particular organs. To do this, an acupuncturist must understand the relation of *Chi* flow to the seasons and the time of day, as well as the interrelationship of the channels.

In the case of non-organ problems, such as muscle pain or a joint injury, the acupuncturist will usually needle cavities near the injury which are not on the channels (remember, almost half the known cavities are not located on channels). This kind of treatment will increase the *Chi* circulation in the injured area and remove the stagnant *Chi*.

This has been only the briefest of introductions to the principles of acupuncture. The author hopes that the *Chi Kung* practitioner is able to gain a basic knowledge of *Chi* circulation. If the reader is interested in further research, there are many books available. The following are suggested:

1. *The Theoretical Foundation of Chinese Medicine Systems of Correspondence,* by Manfred Porkert. MIT Press, Cambridge, Massachusetts and London, 1978.

2. *Acupuncture A Comprehensive Text,* Shanghai College of Traditional Medicine. Translated and edited by John O'Connor and Dan Bensky, Eastland Press, Chicago, 1981.

4-4. Massage and Rubbing

Massage

People have always instinctively rubbed sore muscles and other painful areas to ease their pain and to help the sore muscle recover more quickly.

Long ago it was found that this kind of rubbing can cure a number of disorders such as headaches, joint pain, and uneasy stomach, and that simple rubbing can even strengthen weakened organs.

Massage has been known world-wide. The Japanese have used acupressure, which is derived from Chinese massage, for centuries. The Greek upper classes have used a form of massage, slapping the skin with switches, to cure various disorders. However, the Chinese have fully systematized massage to agree with the theory of *Chi* circulation.

There are three categories of Chinese massage. The first is massaging the muscle: the second, massaging the cavities, or acupuncture points; and the third, massaging the nerve and channel endings. Each category of massage has its own specific uses, but generally a mixture of the three is used.

Massaging the muscles is used to relieve soreness and bruises. The masseuse follows the direction of the muscle fiber using the techniques of: rubbing, pressing, sliding, grasping, slapping, and shaking. The result is an increase in the circulation of blood and *Chi* on the skin and in the muscle area. It also helps to spread accumulated acid, which collects in the muscles due to hard exercise, or blood (in the case of bruises), or stagnant *Chi*, allowing the circulation to disperse them more quickly. Commonly this type of massage is also used to help a person overcome a feeling of weakness or tiredness.

The second category of massage is massaging the acupuncture points. These same points are used in Japanese acupressure, with the addition of a few other points. The principle of massaging the acupuncture points is the same as in acupuncture theory, which is to stimulate the channels by stimulating cavities that can be reached easily by rubbing or pressing with the hands, rather than needles. In acupressure some non-channel points are used to stimulate the local minor *Chi* channels to help circulate energy locally. Figs. 4-7 through 4-12 show the common acupuncture points used in massage.

The third category of massage is to rub or press the endings of the nerves and *Chi* channels. These channels are located on the hands (Fig. 4-13), feet (Fig. 4-14), and ears (Fig. 4-5). One can easily rub with a circular motion the zones which correspond to the different organs, or which are effective for specific symptoms or illnesses. This form of massage is known in the West as reflexology. Theoretically, if the channel endings are rubbed, the *Chi* will be stimulated to a higher level, which will increase the circulation and benefit the related organ or cure the illness.

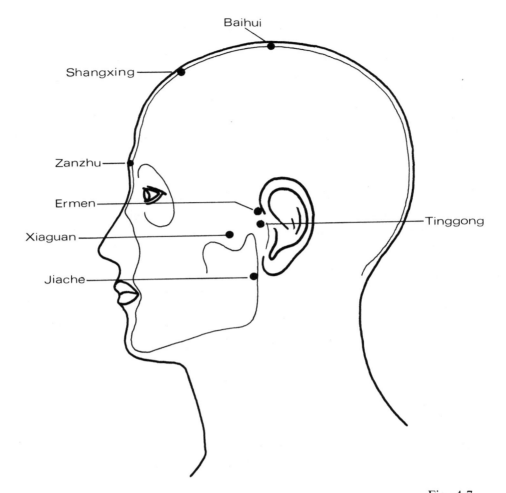

Fig. 4-7.

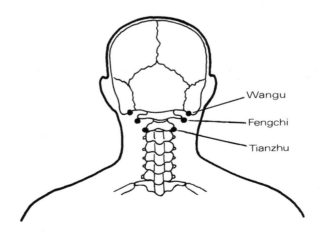

Fig. 4-8.

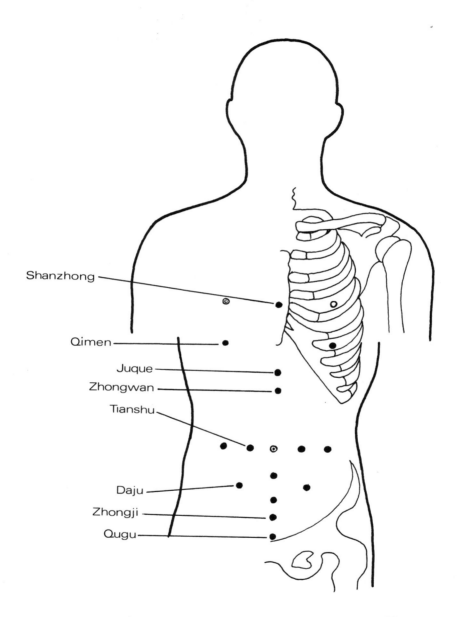

Shanzhong

Qimen

Juque

Zhongwan

Tianshu

Daju

Zhongji

Qugu

Fig. 4-9.

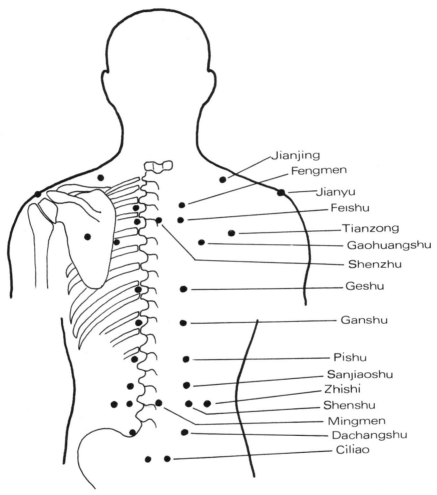

Jianjing
Fengmen
Jianyu
Feishu
Tianzong
Gaohuangshu
Shenzhu
Geshu
Ganshu
Pishu
Sanjiaoshu
Zhishi
Shenshu
Mingmen
Dachangshu
Ciliao

Fig. 4-10.

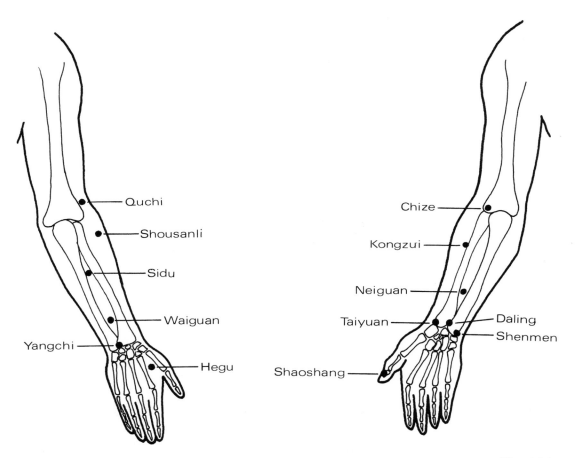

Quchi

Shousanli

Sidu

Waiguan

Yangchi

Hegu

Chize

Kongzui

Neiguan

Taiyuan

Daling

Shenmen

Shaoshang

Fig. 4-11.

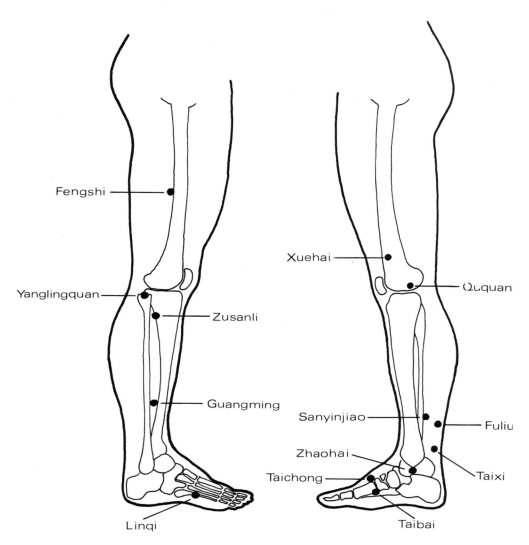

Fig. 4-12.

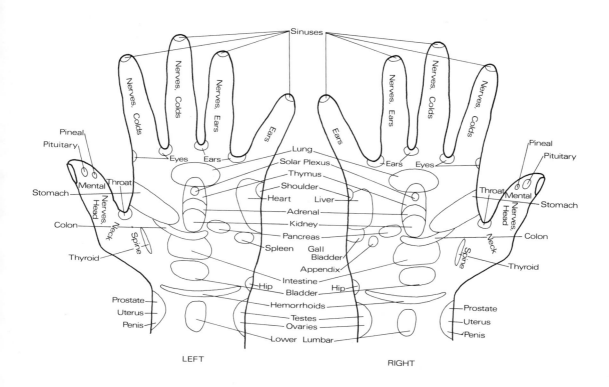

Sinuses

Nerves, Colds
Nerves, Colds
Nerves, Ears
Ears
Ears
Nerves, Ears
Nerves, Colds
Nerves, Colds

Pineal
Pituitary

Eyes
Ears
Lung
Solar Plexus
Thymus
Shoulder
Heart
Liver
Adrenal
Kidney
Pancreas
Spleen
Gall
Bladder
Appendix
Intestine
Hip
Bladder
Hemorrhoids
Testes
Ovaries
Lower Lumbar

Ears
Eyes

Pineal
Pituitary

Throat
Mental
Stomach
Nerves, Head
Colon
Neck
Spine
Thyroid

Prostate
Uterus
Penis

Hip

Throat
Mental
Nerves, Head
Stomach
Neck
Colon
Spine
Thyroid

Prostate
Uterus
Penis

LEFT

RIGHT

Fig. 4-13.

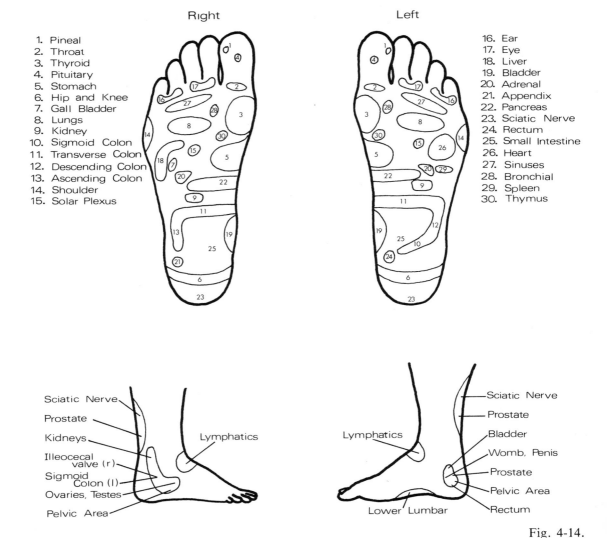

Right

1. Pineal
2. Throat
3. Thyroid
4. Pituitary
5. Stomach
6. Hip and Knee
7. Gall Bladder
8. Lungs
9. Kidney
10. Sigmoid Colon
11. Transverse Colon
12. Descending Colon
13. Ascending Colon
14. Shoulder
15. Solar Plexus

Left

16. Ear
17. Eye
18. Liver
19. Bladder
20. Adrenal
21. Appendix
22. Pancreas
23. Sciatic Nerve
24. Rectum
25. Small Intestine
26. Heart
27. Sinuses
28. Bronchial
29. Spleen
30. Thymus

Sciatic Nerve
Prostate
Kidneys
Illeocecal
    valve (r)
Sigmoid
    Colon (l)
Ovaries, Testes
Pelvic Area
Lymphatics

Sciatic Nerve
Prostate
Bladder
Womb, Penis
Prostate
Pelvic Area
Rectum
Lymphatics
Lower Lumbar

Fig. 4-14.

Hand Forms and Common Methods Used in Massage

Knuckles-single, double, and four fingers for circular rubbing and pressing (Figs. 4-15 through 4-17)

Side of the fist for circular rubbing (Fig. 4-18)

Fingertips for tapping and circular rubbing (Fig. 4-19)

Root of the palm (Base of the thumb) for circular and straight rubbing and pressing (Figs. 4-20 and 4-21)

Base of the fingers for circular and straight rubbing and pressing (Figs. 4-22 and 4-23)

Side of the palm for pressing and rubbing (Fig. 4-24)

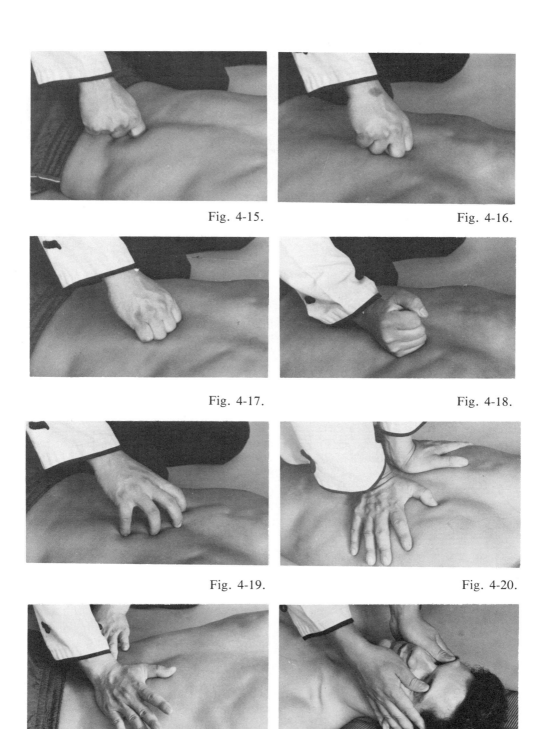

Fig. 4-15.

Fig. 4-16.

Fig. 4-17.

Fig. 4-18.

Fig. 4-19.

Fig. 4-20.

Fig. 4-21.

Fig. 4-22.

Elbow for circular rubbing and pressing (Fig. 4-25)

Fingers for grasping muscles (Figs. 4-26 through 4-29)

Pinching the skin and shaking (Fig. 4-30)

Slapping with the back or the side of the hand (Figs. 4-31 and 4-32)

Rubbing

Very often, when you have an injury such as a bruise or strained joint, you will automatically use the hand to rub the injured area. This rubbing will reduce the pain and ease the nerves and muscles. Theoretically, this kind or rubbing will cause the Chi to circulate, which in turn will prevent stagnation of Chi in that area because of the injury.

In Chi Kung, rubbing or friction is used to increase heat or Chi on the skin, which increases the energy potential there and causes Chi to circulate deeper into the body. Rubbing the face correctly can help greatly in keeping the skin looking youthful, by keeping it well nourished with the flow of Chi and blood. As was mentioned earlier, some parts of the body such as the palm (Fig. 4-13) and the sole of the foot (Fig. 4-14) have channels ending there and rubbing these spots will increase the energy flow in the channels and benefit the corresponding organs. This is different from massaging the channel zones which was described in the previous section. A good example of this is that rubbing the palms together briskly in cold weather will not just keep the arms and hands warm, but the internal organs as well.

Rubbing the skin over some of the organs will increase the function of the organs through the local energy flow caused by the rubbing. For example, rubbing the stomach will lessen pain and increase digestion. Rubbing will also relax the nerves in the area. The same principle holds true for the kidneys.

The large joints of the body: shoulders, elbows, wrists, knees, and ankles are easily injured by overexercise or too much stress on the ligaments. When such injuries do not heal completely, arthritis commonly results. Rubbing the joint area will relax the joint area while stimulating energy circulation, which helps the injured area to heal. In addition, rubbing may even help to cure arthritis after it has set in.

Rubbing methods appropriate to each area of the body:

Face: Rub the eyelids and eyesockets with the fingertips lightly, with a circular motion. Rub the cheeks with light strokes of the fingertips from the nose outward to the sides of the face (Fig. 4-33).

Stomach: Use a circular motion to harmonize with the curve of the intestines (Fig. 4-34).

Foot: Rub and press the zones shown in Fig. 4-14 (Fig. 4-35).

Hand: Rub and press the zones shown in Fig. 4-13 (Fig. 4-36).

Kidney: Rub with a circular motion using the sides of the palm (Fig. 4-37).

Wrist: For joint rubbing, the main purpose is to warm it, not to stimulate the muscles. Rub the wrist by stroking it along the direction of the arm and in a circular motion around the joint (Fig. 4-38).

Fig. 4-23.

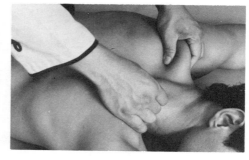

Fig. 4-24.

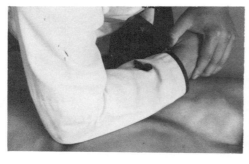

Fig. 4-25.

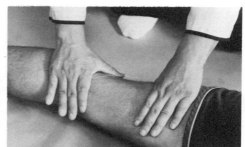

Fig. 4-26.

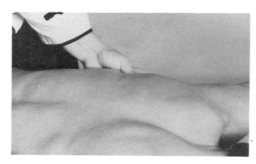

Fig. 4-27.

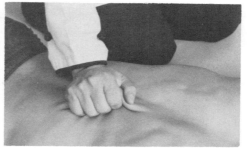

Fig. 4-28.

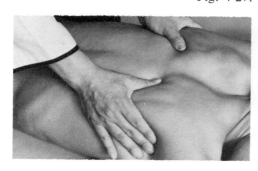

Fig. 4-29.

Fig. 4-30.

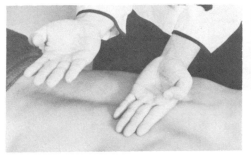

Fig. 4-31.

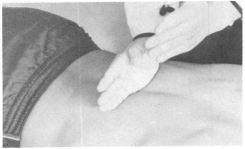

Fig. 4-32.

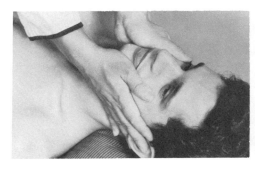

Fig. 4-33.

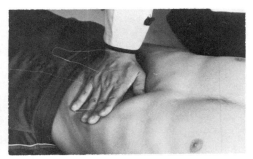

Fig. 4-34.

Fig. 4-35.

Fig. 4-36.

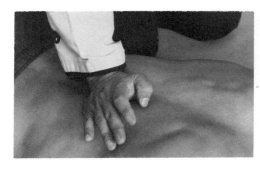

Fig. 4-37.

Fig. 4-38.

Elbow:	Rub lightly both up and down the arm and around the arm (Figs. 4-39 and 4-40).
Shoulder:	Rub lightly both up and down the arm and in a circular motion (Fig. 4-41).
Knee:	Rub lightly both up and down the leg and in a circular motion (Fig. 4-42).
Ankle:	Rub lightly both up and down the leg and around the joint. Also rub and press the zones shown in Fig. 4-14 (Fig. 4-43).

4-5. Miscellaneous Chi Kung Exercises
Swinging the Arms (Bai Bi)

In the last 50 years an exercise developed from the principles of *Yi Gin Ching* has become popular. Although the exercise is very simple, the results in strengthening the body and curing illnesses are very significant. Theoretically, when the arms are swung repeatedly, the nerves and *Chi* channels in the shoulder joints are stimulated to a higher state, and this *Chi* will flow to the areas of lower potential to complete the circulation. Because a number of the *Chi* channels connected with the different organs terminate in the hands, swinging the arms increases the circulation in these channels. Arm swinging will not only increase the *Chi* circulation, but will also increase the flow of blood from the relaxed up and down motion. As a matter of fact, this is the same principle of Wai Dan described in Chapter 2.

From the last 50 years of experience, we know that a number of illnesses can be cured simply by practicing swinging the arms frequently. For some cancers the increase in *Chi* circulation will help the degenerated cells to function normally and eliminate the cancer. According to *Chi* theory, cancers are caused by the stagnation of *Chi* and blood, which results in changes to the structure of the cell. Several types of cancer that can be cured by swinging the arms are cancers of the lungs, esophagus, and lymph. Other kinds of disorders that can also be helped by swinging the arms are: hardening of the liver, paralysis caused by high blood pressure, high blood pressure itself, heart trouble, and nervous disorders.

The method is very simple. Stand with the feet shoulder width apart, with the tip of the tongue touching the roof of the mouth. Swing the arms forward until they are horizontal with the palms facing down (Fig. 4-44), then swing them backwards as far as possible with the palms facing up (Fig. 4-45). Keep the entire body relaxed. Start with 200 to 300 repetitions, then gradually increase to one or two thousand or up to half an hour.

Walking in Place

Many of the channels terminate in the feet and pass through the hip joints. Walking in place has many of the benefits of swinging the arms for similar reasons. As a matter of fact, the reader can do both at the same time.

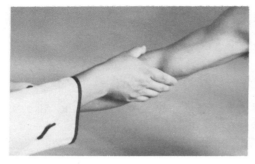

Fig. 4-39.

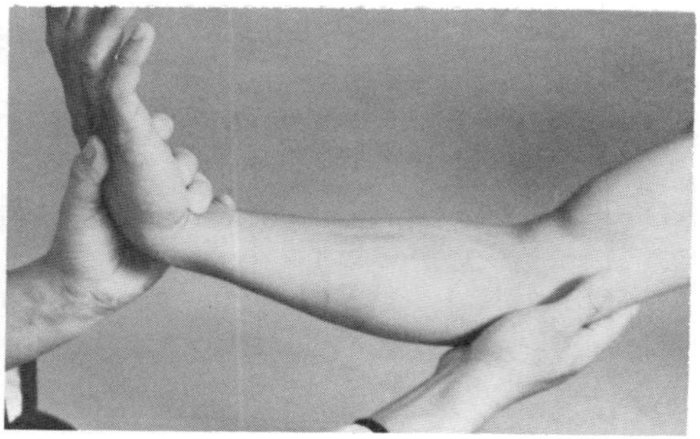

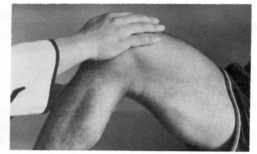

Fig. 4-40.

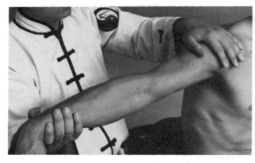

Fig. 4-41.

Fig. 4-42.

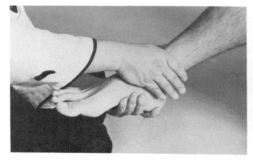

Fig. 4-43.

Fig. 4-44.

Fig. 4-45.   Fig. 4-46.

Treading Bamboo

Stepping on bamboo rods will stimulate the feet where several channel endings are located. This practice is almost like massage, and the principle is the same. In the United States many health stores sell small wooden rollers that are designed for this purpose. Experiments have even shown that this exercise can help some people grow taller.

Exercise Balls

In China one occasionally sees people holding two metal balls the size of ping-pong balls in one hand and rolling them around. This has the same effect as a hand massage. It stimulates and develops the finger and palm muscles and stimulates the reflexology zones (Fig. 4-46) of the palms. The balls are especially good for people who are bedridden and cannot do other exercises.

The Six Sounds

Certain sounds a person makes can affect the circulation of *Chi*. Man has always made sounds when ill or stressed. The sounds are the same for all people around the world. Basically, the function of these sounds is to relieve the interal organs of distress through the lungs. Oriental physicians have investigated the matter scientifically and found that different sounds will affect different organ systems, and high and low tones of a sound will affect the same system differently. Buddhist and Taoist publications describe how different sounds, with varying pitch, are used to relieve or cure several illnesses.

The Taoist documents consulted are: *Tai Sarn Yu Tzou Tzan Ching* by Huang Tian-San, and the *Chen Gin Fan* by Sun Ssu-Mao (581-907 A.D.). The Buddhist texts are the *Shao Tze Kuan* by a Buddhist named Tzu Jee Da Shy of Tian Tai Dson and the *Shan Po Lou Mi* passed down from For Shan (Buddha Mountain).

The following table (Table 4-4) lists the six sounds, their corresponding organ, season, element, external body part, and kind of disorder helped. Both Taoist and Buddhist versions of the sounds are given. The differences may be attributed, in part, to different transliterations of the same Indian Buddhist source text.

The six sounds should be done in one continuous breath. This will cause the chain relaxation of the corresponding organs. Also, the sound should not be loud. When a loud sound is made, the corresponding organ will become tight and this will stagnate the *Chi* circulation. The sounds should be soft, barely audible, and relaxed.

Table 4-4

Taoist	*Hur*	*Fu*	*Hui*	*Shi*	*Shiu*	*Chuei*
Buddhist	*Hur*	*Fu*	*Shyh*	*Shi*	*Shiu*	*Chuei*
Organ	Heart	Spleen	Lung	Triple Burner	Liver	Kidney
Season	Summer	Four Seasons	Autumn	Internal Fire	Spring	Winter
Element	Fire	Earth	Metal	Mutual Fire	Wood	Water
Body Part	Tongue	Stomach	Skin	Chest	Eyes	Ear
Disorders	Heart Burn	Indigestion	Cold Cough	Chest Pain	Burning Liver	Waist Pain
	Dry mouth	Diarrhea			Red Eyes	Joint Pain
	Thirst					

CHAPTER 5
MARTIAL ARTS APPLICATIONS

5-1. Introduction

The Chinese have studied and developed the martial arts for more than 4000 years. In the beginning only limited techniques using brute muscle power were available. It was not until about 200 B.C., when the circulation of *Chi* and the use of acupuncture became well understood, that the martial application of *Chi* began. The attention devoted to it increased significantly when Da Mo's *Wai Dan* exercises began to be used at the Shaolin Temple in 536 A.D. Although the *Yi Gin Ching* exercise was intended to be used only for the improvement of health, the monks found that it greatly increased the strength and efficiency of their muscles. The training also allowed them to direct the *Chi* to parts of their body to resist blows. It was only natural that they applied this to the martial arts. Learning martial arts was a necessity of the time in order to protect the temple property and for traveling. From that time on the use of *Wai Dan* to develop *Chi* and to improve the martial arts has been widely researched and developed.

Once it became know that a balanced, unimpeded flow of *Chi* was necessary for life and well being, the next step was to find ways to affect the enemy's *Chi* flow. Martial arts masters found that of the several hundred acupuncture cavities, 108 can be easily affected by striking, pressing, grabbing, or kicking. Hitting cavities to cause death, unconsciousness or paralysis was called ''cavity strike'' or ''cavity press''. This technique, together with ''sealing the breath or vein'' has been considered the highest art in *Kung Fu*.

Striking the enemy in such a way as to cause either the windpipe to be obstructed or the lungs or diaphragm to be cramped, so the person cannot breathe, is called ''sealing the breath.'' ''Sealing the vein'' means to strike or press cavities so that the supply of blood to the brain is obstructed, causing unconsciousness. In order to give the martial artist the strength to penetrate to the cavities, the hands and fingers were conditioned and trained by such methods as "Iron Sand Palm" and "Secret Sword." Penetration power training methods were also created, such as punching a candle flame and slapping a cloth.

Martial artists who had practiced *Nei Dan* exercises for many years were able to move energy outside their bodies. Using cavities, they were able to put *Chi* into a person's system or take it out. This meant they could do cavity strikes without toughening their bodies and without using much force—perhaps with only a touch. This art has fallen into disuse over the centuries, and there are few people today with this ability.

As mentioned above, *Chi Kung* was also used by the Shaolin monks to toughen the body to an extent that seems incredible to most Westerners. An adept could withstand strong blows, edged weapons, and even cavity press, but not, of course, bullets. In *Kung Fu* this is called "Iron Shirt" *(Tiea Bu Shan)* or "Golden Bell Cover" *(Gin Chung Tsao)*.

In this chapter we will briefly discuss cavity press, sealing the vein, sealing the breath, and Iron Shirt or Golden Bell Cover. The cycle of *Chi* and cavity points will also be briefly discussed. Readers who are interested in more information on cavity location, *Chi* circulation, and cavity press techniques should refer to the author's book *Shaolin Chin Na*. A detailed description of these techniques will require a separate book to explain the training methods, exact location of cavities, anatomy, theory, attacking methods, etc. The author hopes to publish a book on this in the future.

5-2. Cavity Press

The technique of Cavity Press *(Tien Hsueh)* is probably the highest accomplishment of *Chi Kung* in the martial arts. Ever since *Chi* was understood, martial artists have used various methods to affect an enemy's *Chi*, either instantly or with a delayed reaction, with the object of causing death, unconsciousness, stupefaction, or numbness of a body area.

In the course of their researches, Chinese martial artists have found 108 cavities which can be attacked. There are 72 which are considered minor cavities because they cannot be used to kill an opponent, and 36 which are vital cavities because it is possible to kill someone by striking one of them at the right time with the correct force. In striking cavities the time of day must be right for the strike to be effective and the exact spot must be struck. The correct hand form must be used; for example, some cavities can be successfully affected by a strike with the knee while others require a strike with one finger. The force used must be sufficient to affect the channel and penetrate to the right depth because while some cavities are very close to the surface, others are deeper within the body. In order to be effective, therefore, the martial artist must first know acupuncture channels, nerves, and anatomy; second, he must know the theory of *Chi* circulation in relation to time of day; and third he must be trained in hand and leg forms and power development. The martial artist must also know the techniques for curing cavity press attacks. If the enemy is not dead from an attack or if a friend has been attacked, there are techniques for reviving them. In many cases, unconscious people can be revived with just a push, pinch, or massage in the correct spot.

Principles of Cavity Press

Cavity Press is a technique in which the practitioner affects the opponent's *Chi* or blood circulation by striking a cavity with a finger, palm, fist, foot, or elbow, or by grasping. When a cavity is effectively struck, several things can happen:

The strike can affect *Chi* circulation and can cause the failure of the corresponding internal organ. For example, a strike to the armpit, affecting the heart channel, will shock the heart like a blow to the funny bone affects the arm.

The strike can affect both *Chi* circulation and blood circulation. When the cavity is struck, the muscles around it cramp and cut off blood flow. If the force is sufficient and affects an artery, the artery can rupture, usually resulting in death. For example, a strike to the temple will both shock the brain and possibly rupture the carotid artery. A weak blow to the temple cavity will cause unconsciousness.

The strike can directly affect an internal organ. This category of striking is sometimes called *"Chi Kuann Da"* or *"Organ Striking"*. For example, a strike to the solar plexus will shock the heart and can cause death. Another example is a strike to the liver, which can cause the muscles around it to cramp and damage it. Sufficient force will rupture it. The liver and kidneys are especially susceptible to this kind of attack.

For a number of cavities, a strike will not result in any obvious injury. However, the strike in fact causes the *Chi* to stagnate in that area, and the person will become ill or die at some later time, one or two months or even one year in the future. For example, strikes to spinal cavities will generally not show their effect until much later. From anatomy and acupuncture it is known that the spine is the trunk line for the nervous system and the main conduit for *Chi*. If cavities located in the spinal area are injured, the flow of *Chi* to the organ related to that part of the spine will be weakened, and eventually failure of the organ will occur.

There are a number of cavities which can be struck to temporarily disable an enemy. For example, a strike to the *Tianzong* cavity on the shoulder blade will result in the whole shoulder and arm becoming numb. Another example know to everyone, is the funny bone or *Shaohai* cavity.

The last kind of cavity strike stuns the enemy, causing him to be disordered or dizzy or "out on his feet".

Cavity Press and Time

In the human body the main flow of *Chi* and blood changes according to the time of day and the season of the year. Since the body is part of nature, it is natural that it is affected by the forces at work in the environment.

Generally speaking, during the day, the *Chi* flows most strongly in the front of the body, while at night it flows most strongly in the back. At midnight it is concentrated at the head, then its focus moves down the front of the body. It is at the solar plexus at noon and at the perineum at sunset. Then the focus moves up the back and ends at the top of the head again at midnight.

Also, the *Chi* flow moves from one channel to another every two hours, completing a cycle of the twelve main channels every day. The governing and conception vessels are not involved in this cycle. Their flow is constant. Table 5-1 lists the relationship between *Chi* and blood flow and the time of day.

It follows, then, that a martial artist who knows how to coordinate his target with the time of day can easily hurt his opponent in ways that seem mysterious

Table 5-1

TIME	CHANNEL	BODY AREA	CAVITY
Tzyy 11PM-1AM	Gall Bladder	Foot	*Renzhong*
Choou 1AM-3AM	Liver	Waist	*Billiang* or *Meishin*
Yn 3AM-5AM	*Lung*	Eye	*Baihui*
Mao 5AM-7AM	Large Intestine	Face	*Jiache* or *Ya Sha*
Chen 7AM-9AM	Stomach	Head	*Taiyang*
Shy 9AM-11AM	Spleen	Hand	*Yingchuang* or *Gian Tai*
Wuu 11AM-1PM	Heart	Chest	*Neiquan* or *Wan Mei*
Wey 1PM-3PM	Small Intestine	Stomach	*Jiuwei* or *Hsin Kan*
Shen 3PM-5PM	Bladder	Heart	*Qihai* or *Dan Tien*
Yeou 5PM-7PM	Kidney	Back (Spleen)	*Jimen* or *Bai Hai*
Shiu 7PM-9PM	Pericardium	Neck (Head)	*Sha Yin*
Hay 9PM-11PM	Triple Burner	Leg (Ankle)	*Yongquan*

to the uninitiated. Because he attacks the most intense energies of the body at that particular time, the injury is immediate and drastic.

It was found that there are twelve major cavities which are particularly sensitive to attack at specific times. These cavities and their striking times are also listed in Table 5-1, and their locations are illustrated in Figs. 5-1 through 5-7. Furthermore, it was discovered that the *Chi* flow was more predominant in various parts of the body throughout the day. Table 5-1 lists the parts of the body and their times of greatest *Chi* flow.

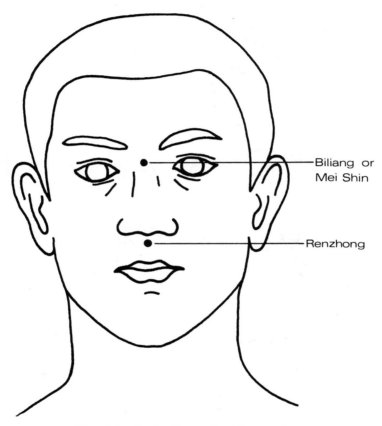

Biliang or
Mei Shin

Renzhong

Fig. 5-1. Cavity Press Cavities on the Face

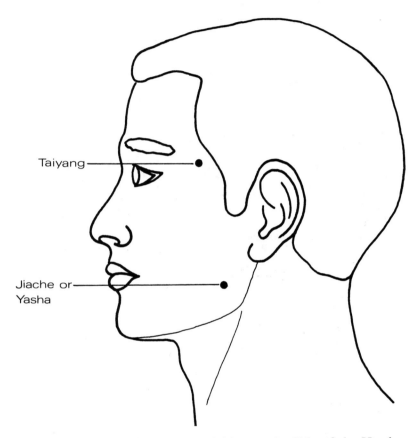

Fig. 5-2. Cavity Press Cavities on the Side of the Head

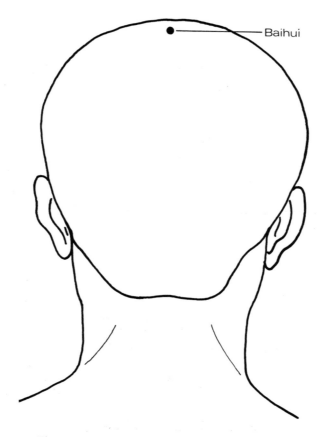

Baihui

Fig. 5-3. Cavity Press Cavity on the Crown

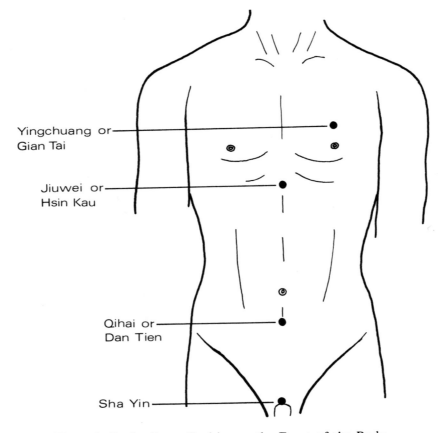

Yingchuang or
Gian Tai

Jiuwei or
Hsin Kau

Qihai or
Dan Tien

Sha Yin

Fig. 5-4. Cavity Press Cavities on the Front of the Body

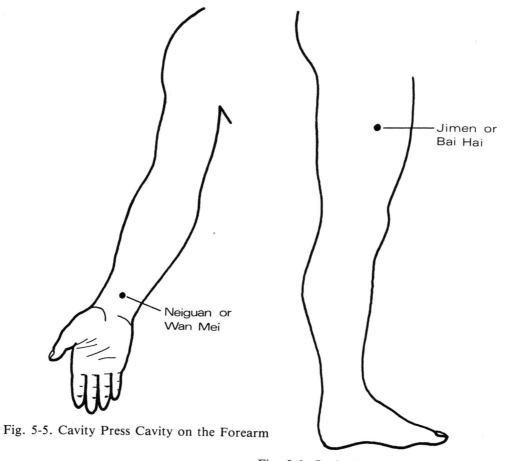

Fig. 5-5. Cavity Press Cavity on the Forearm

Neiguan or
Wan Mei

Jimen or
Bai Hai

Fig. 5-6. Cavity Press Cavity on the Thigh

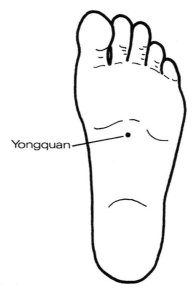

Yongquan

Fig. 5-7. Cavity Press Cavity on the Bottom of the Foot

5-3. Sealing the Vein and Sealing the Breath
Sealing the Vein (Duan Mie)

Strictly speaking, sealing the vein can also be classified as a cavity press because the vein is sealed by striking a cavity. It is considered separately from cavity press by Chinese martial artists because the injury principle is different. In sealing the vein, the main principle is to cause unconsciousness or even death by stopping the flow of blood to the head, cutting off the oxygen supply to the brain. Therefore, it is easy to understand that the cavities that are used for sealing the vein are mainly located in the neck.

There are two principal ways to seal the vein: striking and compression. When certain cavities on the neck near the carotid artery are struck, it will affect the *Chi* circulation in that area and shock the nerves around the cavity. This will in turn cause the muscle to spasm, blocking the artery and completely or partially sealing the blood supply to the brain. When a person does not receive oxygen to the brain for 5-10 seconds, he will lose consciousness. Another way of sealing the vein is to compress the side of the neck by choking to seal the artery and stop the oxygen supply.

The person whose vein has been sealed can be revived within a few minutes without damage to the brain. Usually, a palm strike to a certain spot on the spine will release the muscle tension in the neck and allow the blood to flow freely again. After the person is revived, a soft massage of the neck muscles will expedite the recovery.

Sealing the Breath (Bi Chi)

Sealing the breath is a technique which causes a person to lose consciousness by restricting the supply of air to the lungs so that the person cannot breathe. There are two main categories of sealing the breath. In one, the wind pipe is sealed by being grasped and compressed, which completely stops the air from being taken into the lungs, thus causing unconsciousness or even death. In the other, the channels around the lungs or the channels which are associated with the lungs are struck. The lungs are protected by the ribs, which are covered with layers of muscles inside and outside. In an ordinary strike, only the muscles on the outside of the ribs are affected. However, if the appropriate cavity on the chest or back is struck, the muscles inside the ribs will also be shocked. They will tighten up and prevent the lungs from expanding and taking in air. Usually this type of sealing the breath will cause only a partial sealing of the lungs. Most of the time the person will lose consciousness because of lack of oxygen but will not die. If an injured person is not revived for a long time, death might result. But generally the person will recover by himself. To speed recovery, apply pressure with the palm to the side of the chest that is not in spasm. This will balance the pressure and help to release the spasm. The person can also be revived by throwing water on him.

Sealing the breath can be effected by striking the cavities just above and below the nipple, the solar plexus, the stomach muscles, or any of several cavities on the back.

5-4. Golden Bell Cover or Iron Shirt

Chinese martial artists often demonstrate their prowess by bending an iron bar pressed into their throats. They do this by concentrating *Chi* at the spot the bar is pressing. This is a spectacular way of demonstrating the results of a martial *Chi Kung* training system called "Iron Shirt" *(Tiea Bu Shan)* or "Golden Bell Cover" *(Gin Chung Tsao)*. The reason for these names is that the training will enable a person to resist a blow or punch without injury or pain, as though he were wearing an iron shirt or were protected by a golden bell.

This training may have started in the sixth century when Da Mo's *Yi Gin Ching* began to be used for training. One of the main efforts of *Yi Gin Ching* training is to concentrate the *Chi* in a specific area, which will not only increase the muscle power, which is supported by *Chi*, but will also increase the ability to resist blows, reducing injury to a minimum. This kind of training has continued to be researched and practiced until the present. Because the training of the body's resistance comes from repeated beating, it is also called "Beating Endurance" *(Ai Da)* training. Another name of this training is "Bunch Beating" *(Pie Da)* because the first few stages of training consist of using bunches of bamboo, wood, and iron wire to hit the body.

The principle of the training is very simple. The reader probably has had the experience before, that if the appropriate muscle is tightened when some part of the body is hit, the pain and injury will be reduced. That is the beginning of Iron Shirt training. The reason for this phenomenon is that when muscles are tight, the *Chi* flow is slowed down so that the nerve sensation is slow and dull. This will stop the pain message from passing to the brain. Additionally, when the muscles are tensed up, the power of a blow or punch will be mostly stopped by the tensed muscle, so the main *Chi* channels under the muscles won't be disturbed. Consequently the injury will be confined to the muscle itself, not to the organs related to the *Chi* channel.

In order to prevent injury the practitioner must be conditioned gradually, first his skin and then his muscles. Then in advanced "Iron Shirt" the *Chi* must be trained to concentrate in the punched area to repulse the punch. With the *Chi* supporting the muscle, the *Chi* channel won't be injured, and so the body can eventually resist even a cavity press. Therefore, in order to complete the advanced training, the *Chi Kung Wai Dan* training from Chapter 2 is extremely important. Also, in order to keep the *Chi* circulation smooth and complete, *Nei Dan* should also be practiced. Without *Wai Dan* and *Nei Dan* training the "Iron Shirt" will be only on the surface of the body. The body can still be injured when attacked by penetrating power.

There is a martial proverb: "Train the muscles and skin externally, and train *Chi* internally". This implies that *Chi Kung* is the foundation of the training. *Chi* training can make the internal organs strong and healthy. When *Chi* is concentrated by the mind, it can be expanded to the entire body (see Chapter 3) or focused in a small area to rebound a blow.

In Iron Shirt training, the first step is to beat the skin with minor power with bamboo or rattan strips about one and a half feet long, bound at one end. This striking will stimulate mainly the skin and surface muscles. Because no deep injury can occur, the entire body can be trained in this way. However, for the very beginner, only areas which have a thick layer of muscle to support the blows, the shoulders, stomach, chest, back, thighs, arms, and calves, should be struck. With each strike, the muscle being struck should be tightened and the mind should be concentrated at that spot. This will train the *Chi* concentration and the natural resistant reaction. Only after the above areas can take the strike without feeling pain can other areas such as the shins, knees, head, elbows, etc., be trained. This training should be continued until the practitioner does not feel pain.

This skin and shallow muscle stimulation will let the nerve system get acclimated to being struck. If a ticklish person were tickled constantly, pretty soon his nerve system would no longer feel ticklish. This training works the same way.

The next step is to use striking power which can penetrate deeper. For this training, a bunch of iron wire, bound at one end is used. Follow the same routine with *Chi* concentration and muscle tension until the deep muscles can resist the external blows. For this step, since the blow will be stronger and more penetrating, the practitioner must have strong *Chi* to avoid disturbing the *Chi* flow. Also, herbs should be used to cure the bruises, so that *Chi* will not become stagnant anywhere.

It is important to note here that all these training methods should be done only with a qualified master who knows how to control the penetration power of the blows, and who also knows how to treat injuries.

Only after the less dangerous areas have been trained, and the practitioner has gained enough skill with *Chi* transport, can other vital areas such as the head, throat, kidneys and liver be trained. Also at this point, the master will start to stimulate the vital cavities such as the temples, throat, armpits, solar plexus, etc. to train the student to protect these areas. Later, these vital cavities will be struck at their most vulnerable times of day. When a practitioner can resist a cavity press to a vital area without pain and injury, then he has completed his training.

There are two vital places, the eyes and the groin where *Chi* cannot be directed. Therefore, they remain vulnerable even for someone who has completed the above training. However, there are some practitioners who are able to pull their testicles up into the abdomen, leaving only their eyes vulnerable.

CHAPTER 6
CONCLUSION

The author hopes that this book will help to set people on the right path of *Chi Kung* research and development, and will dispel some of the mystery and confusion which still shroud this art.

This book can be only a beginning. It is now up to you, the reader, to practice and research for yourself.

The information in this book will enable you to lay a good foundation in energy development. Space has limited our presentation of the martial applications of *Chi Kung*, but the author hopes to publish more information on this matter in the future. For the health and healing aspects of *Chi Kung*, the reader will have to seek out other more qualified teachers. The author hopes that he has provided the general reader with a useful overview of this ancient and useful Chinese art.

A-1. **A Poem by Lu Yu About Da Mo**

宋陸游為達磨詩

亦不觀惡而生嫌。
亦不觀善而勤措。
亦不捨智而近愚。
亦不抛迷而就悟。
達大道今過量，
通佛心今出度，
不與凡聖同經，
超然名之曰祖。

從來為長神生動不行，

氣身形以養，長不出而勤。

入離可以行欲心不勤。

經結，

氣去氣無氣若。注來在路。

息中。神神虛則。

胎氣息，知守行住相無常道

伏中生。固神氣氣去然真

自胎之死，則神無自是

胎有為之生氣住，念入之

APPENDIX B

TRANSLATION OF CHINESE TERMS

ABOUT THE AUTHOR

武術 Wushu
功夫 Kung Fu
白鶴 Pai Huo
曾金灶 Cheng Gin-Gsao
高濤 Kao Tao
台北 Taipei
淡江學院 Tamkang College
長拳 Chang Chuan
李茂清 Li Mao-Ching
國術 Kuoshu
擒拿 Chin Na

PREFACE

氣功 Chi Kung
氣 Chi
太極拳 Tai Chi Chuan
外丹 Wai Dan
少林 Shaolin
達磨 Da Mo
易筋經 Yi Gin Ching
內丹 Nei Dan
丹田 Dan Tien
楊俊敏 Yang Jwing-Ming

CHAPTER ONE

內功 Nei Kung
氣化論 Chi Far Lun
經絡論 Gin Lou Lun
經 Gin
絡 Lou
穴 Hsueh
陰 Yin
陽 Yang
金 Gin
木 Moo
水 Sui
火 For
土 Tu
外象解剖 Wai Shain Gieh Por
內視功夫 Nei Shih Fung Fu
天時 Tien Shih
地理 Di Li
人事 Zen Shih

斯 Shih
噓 Shiu
嘿 Hai
哈 Ha
八段錦 Ba Dun Gin
十二段錦 Shih Er Dun Gin
達磨易筋經 Da Mo Yi Gin Ching
行意 Hsing I
六合八法 Liu Ho Ba Fa
李白 Li Pai
蘇東坡 Su Tung-Pou
白居易 Bai Gue-Yi
沈仔中 Shen Tsun-Chung
蘇沈良方 Su Shen Lian Fan
漢 Han
黃帝 Huang Di
商 Shang
砭石 Bian Shih
內經素問 Nei Ching Su Wen
易經 I Ching
老子 Lao Tzu
李耳 Li Erh
道德經 Tao Te Ching
史記 Shih Gi
莊子 Chuang Tzu
秦 Chin
難經 Nan Ching
扁鵲 Bian Chiueh
漢書藝文誌 Han Su Yin Wun Tzu
金匱要略 Gin Guey Yao Liueh
張仲景 Chang Chung-Gien
周易參同契 Chou Yi Chan Ton Chi
魏伯陽 Wei Bo-Yang
晉 Gin
華陀情戲 Hua Tor
君倩 Juan Gin
五禽戲 Wu Chin Si
洪 Gar Hung
抱朴子 Bao Poh Tzu
陶弘景 Tao Hung-Gin
養性延命錄 Yang Shen Yen Ming Lu
梁 Liang

達磨	Da Mo
隋	Sui
唐	Tang
方論	Chow Yun-Fan
諸病源候論	Chu Bin Yun Hou Lun
千金方	Chen Gin Fan
孫思邈	Sun Ssu-Mao
外台祕要	Wai Tai Mi Yao
王燾	Wang Tor
宋	Sung
金	Gin
元	Yuan
養生訣	Yang Shen Gieh
張安道	Chang An-Tao
儒門視事	Zu Men Shih Shih
張子和	Chang Tzu-Huo
蘭室祕藏	Lan Shih Mi Chan
李果	Li Gou
格致餘論	Ge Tzi Yu Lun
朱丹溪	Chu Dan-Si
張三丰	Chang San-Feng
武當	Wu Dan
王唯一	Wang Wei-Yi
清	Ching
岳飛	Yeuh Fei
峨嵋	Er Mei
四川	Sichuan
虎步功	Fu Bu Kung
十二莊	Shih Er Chuan
叫化功	Giaou Far Kung
明	Ming
奇經八脈考	Chi Ching Ba Mei Kou
李時珍	Li Shih-Tsin
保身祕要	Bao Shen Mi Yao
曹元白	Tso Yun-Bai
養生餘語	Yang Shen Huo Yu
陳繼儒	Chen Gi-Zu
精	Gien
神	Shen
醫方集解	Yi Fan Gi Gieh
汪訒庵	Wong Fan-Yen
王祖源	Wang Tzu-Yun
內功圖說	Nei Kung Tuo Shou
火龍功	For Long Kung
太陽	Tai Yang
少海	Shaohai
手少陰心經	Shaoyin Heart Channel
任脈	Ren Mei
督脈	Du Mei

十三勢拳	Shih Shan Shih
綿拳	Mei Chuan
長拳	Chang Chuan
楊露禪	Yang Lu-Shan
陳長興	Chen Chang-Shen
楊班候	Yang Pan-Huo
吳全佑	Wu Chun-Yu
吳鑑泉	Wu Chien-Chun
楊澄甫	Yang Chen-Fu
董海川	Tung Hai-Chuan
文安	Wen An
河北	Hebei
九華山	Giou Hwa Mountain
畢澄霞	Bi Dern-Shai
姬隆豐	Gi Long-Fon
山西	Shanxi
拳經	Chuan Ching
終南山	Tsong Nan Mountain
五行拳	Wu Hsing Chuan
十大形	Shih Da Hsing
十二形	Shih Er Hsing
八式	Ba Shih
雜式捶	Gar Shih Chuan
十二橫捶	Shih Er Hen Chuan
出洞	Chu Zu Don
安身炮	An Shen Pou
絞山炮	Giau Shan Pou
王花炮	Wu Fa Pou
陳博	Chen Bou
華山	Hua Shan
氣	Chi
骨	Ku
形	Hsing
隨	Hsui
提	Ti
還	Huan
勒	Le
伏	Fu

CHAPTER TWO

丹功	Gin Dan
散功	San Kung
利	Sardili
乘	Shan Sheng
大乘	Da Sheng
中乘	Chung Sheng
小乘	Shao Sheng
梁武	Liang Wu
光孝寺	Kuan Shao Temple
廣東	Canton

昂岩	Shaou Yon
少室山山	Shao Shih Mountain
嵩山	Sonn Mountain
登封縣	Teng Fon Hsien
河南	Henan
魏	Wei
跋陀法師	Pao Jaco
游陸	Lu Yu
搭橋	Da Chiao
鐵板橋	Tiea Bann Chiao
童子拜佛	Ton Tzu Bai For
托天	Tou Tian

CHAPTER THREE

張三丰	Chang San-Feng
武當山	Wu Dan Mountain
鐘縣	Chun Hsien
湖北	Hubei
食氣	Yang Chi
生禪	Tsao Chan
鍊氣	Lien Chi
運氣	Yun Chi
行氣	Hsing Chi
運功	Yun Kung
行功	Hsing Kung
丹田	Dan Tien
胎息	Tai Shih
氣海	Qihai
火爐	For Lu
胎息經	Tai Shih Ching
返童	Fan Ton
起火	Chi For
意守丹田	Yi Sou Dan Tien
動膃	Don Chu
任脈	Ren Mei
督脈	Du Mei
搭橋	Da Chiao
天池	Tien Tzie
龍泉	Lung Chuan
小週天	Shao Chou Tien
三關	San Guan
尾閭	Wei Lu
長强	Changqiang
閟肛	Bi Gang
鬆肛	Shon Gang
命門	Ming Men
夾脊	Jar Gi
靈台	Lingtai
玉枕	Yu Gen
腦戶	Nao Hu

反呼吸	Fan Fu Shih
正呼吸	Tzan Fu Shih
鳴鼓	Min Gu
叩齒	Kou Tshi
上屑氣	Shar Chen Chi
下屑氣	Sarn Chen Chi
充氣	Chun Chi
撮氣	Kuar Chi
拱手	Gung Sou

CHAPTER FOUR

陰	Yin
陽	Yang
望診	Wang Chen
聞診	Wen Chen
問診	Wenn Chen
切診	Chei Chen
經	Ching
絡	Lou
奇經八脈	Chi Ching Ba Mei
三焦	Sanjiao
太陰	Taiyin
少陰	Shaoyin
厥陰	Jueyin
太陽	Taiyang
少陽	Shaoyang
陽明	Yangming
擺臂	Bai Bi
太上玉軸真經	Tai Sarn Yu Tzou Tzan Ching
黃庭	Huang Tian-San
千金方	Chen Gin Fan
孫思邈	Sun Ssu-Mao
小止觀	Shao Tze Kuan
智者大師	Tzu Jee Da Shy
天台宗	Tian Tai Dson
禪波羅蜜	Shan Po Lou Mi
佛山	For Shan
呵	Hur
呼	Fu
咽	Hui
呬	Shyh
嘻	Shi
噓	Shiu
吹	Chuei

CHAPTER FIVE

鐵布衫	Tiea Bu Shan
金鐘罩	Gin Chung Tsao
點穴	Tien Hsueh
巽官打客	Chi Kuann Da
天宗	Tianzong

少海　Shaohai
閉氣　Bi Chi
斷脈　Duan Mie
挨打　Ai Da
排打　Pie Da